Relate! Transforming Our Relationship With The Earth

Lionel Berube

Also by Lionel Berube

Connect! Getting In Touch With Self, Consciousness, and Cosmos

Shift! Small Changes in Thinking Can Have Big Effects on Living

February, 2018
Lionel Berube
Relate! Transforming Our Relationship With The Earth
ISBN 10 is 1985723700 and ISBN 13 is 9781985723702

Special Thanks to Elinor Berube, Karen Angel, and Elaine
Casey.
They made this a better book.

Contents

A Fresh Perspective

Whether change is personal or social, it is usually difficult and often seems impossible. In matters of major social change, people try to do the right action, yet find that for all their efforts, the conditions remain the same. David Suzuki, long a warrior for the ecological restoration of the planet wrote, "In the 1970s and '80s, environmentalists celebrated after stopping dams, supertanker traffic along coasts and drilling in critical areas, only to find they had to fight the same battles again 30 or 40 years later. In other words, what seemed like victories had turned out to be pyrrhic because we failed to shift the way people see the world."[1] And therein lies the problem, that is, how does one move the discussion from merely acting to rectify a situation to a real transformation in perspective that makes meaningful change a natural outcome? The historical truth is that unless there is such a transformation, nothing will amount to more than superficial change or window dressing. Engaging in manipulating signs and symbols won't do. To make a real and significant difference, we need to transform the deep roots of our thinking. In a way, our condition is much like the person who changes clothes often enough but doesn't ever wash. Sooner or later basic issues will surface and no amount of changing clothes will have any effect at all. To effect a significant change in how we treat the Earth, something fundamental in the way we experience our relationship to the planet, the attitudes we have toward other living entities, and our assumptions about our place in the scheme of things merits a serious inquiry.

If we are truly concerned with making this Earth the beautiful place where we all want to live, we will have to modify our self-image as a species as we reconnect with the Earth. If we don't transform our self-image, the drug problem, environmental destruction, nuclear stockpiling, and all the rest of the world's ills, they will continue to play havoc with our vision of what is possible. All of our efforts will continue to be pyrrhic, that is, a failed victory.

The good news is that we are on the way to the necessary transformation in human consciousness that may well bring about the necessary changes in our civilization. As with all major social changes, each of us is free to choose a part to play if we want to act in our collective best interests. Perhaps a first step is a willingness to alter not only our conscious philosophy, but the largely unconscious underpinning historical philosophy. In a way, each of us has one idea encapsulated within another and out of sight, much like a Russian doll, called a matryoshka. The doll is a set of wooden dolls of decreasing size placed one inside the other. Our philosophical ideas are much the same. As Rebecca Goldstein reminds us, "Philosophical progress is invisible because it is incorporated into our points of view… We don't see it, because we see with it."[2] Here it is worth noting Shakespeare's Hamlet communicating his understanding to Horatio: "There are more things in heaven and earth than are dreamt of in our philosophy." With that in mind, let's take a brief look at two different and powerful views of our place in the universe. And following that, let's look at where we can incorporate both views in a new vision of our place within and on the planet.

Within most, if not all, indigenous cultures and pre-agricultural societies, humans were seen as embedded within a living natural world; virtually everything was pregnant with meaning and purpose. The boundary between people and the natural environment was porous, that is, people were connected psychically and physically to their surroundings. The interior world of the human was continuous with the universe. The world was ensouled and enchanted. Spirit was omnipresent in all things. People were part and parcel of all that is. There was no clear division between human and other life entities; we were all part of the world soul. All life was embedded in a larger mystery. The Earth's character might be described as Nietzsche said in another connection, "The world is deep, deeper than day can comprehend."

In contrast, now we see ourselves as disconnected from an inert, non-living world. Humans are autonomous, self-aware, self-actualizing, and self-determined. Only humans have value, purpose, and meaning. The Earth is disenchanted, without meaning, purpose, consciousness or value. To ascribe any of these properties to anything else beyond human beings is simply projecting our own stuff. There is no world soul, only matter and energy. The Earth exists for us to exploit at will to serve our needs alone. Humans stand alone, utterly without purpose in a stark, meaningless universe.

The beginnings of a third perspective is coming into view. In this new vision, we honor all that is about us and use our capacity as humans to extend our relationship of care, consideration, respect, and love to what nourishes us – the Earth, or as it is affectionally known by many, Gaia. We have come to recognize that we are connected in every possible way, that we are not alone in having meaning, purpose, and value, that the Earth can speak to us, that we are co-creators of our earthly condition, that we are participants in the on-going evolutionary drama affecting all life on the planet.

The inescapable contrast between the two earlier, basic perspectives is beginning to crack. One of the heralds of a new contemporary view is the late Terrence McKenna, a Harvard-trained scientist who spent years studying exotic plants and indigenous cultures. He wrote, "Nature is not mute, but modern man is deaf – made deaf because he is unwilling to hear the message of caring, balance, and cooperation that is nature's message. In our state of denial we must proclaim nature mute – how else to avoid facing the awful crimes we have committed for centuries against nature and each other. The Nazis said that Jews were not true human beings and that their mass murder was thus not of any consequence. Some industrialists and politicians use a similar dis-ensouling argument to excuse the destruction of the planet, the maternal matrix necessary to all life."[3] McKenna is unequivocal in his assertion that we must move beyond our current disenchanted views and embrace our connection with all life on Earth. "If we do not learn from our past, this story could end with a planet toxified, its forest a memory, it biological cohesion shattered, our birth legacy a weed-choked wasteland." Nature is our beloved, meant to be cherished and explored, not raped and conquered. In his and other's view, we need to get beyond traditional monotheism and standard scientific reductionism -- both whose complete indifference to the soul and mind of the natural world has brought us to the precipice of ecological disaster.

Of course, we are not going to change our perspectives overnight or without some serious re-thinking of our place in the universe. However, we are now in a position to consider a re-evaluation. Indeed, "We are trapped in our own personal history that is in turn nested inside our cultural and national history, and that in turn is embedded in biological, evolutionary, geological, and cosmological history. It's not going to end today, or tomorrow… Like an insect stuck in amber, we are imprisoned in time, and rather than waste energy trying to escape… we should rather devote our efforts to making the time we are afforded the best it can possibly be."[4]

As part of that re-evaluation, we do well to reflect on Martin Buber's "I-It" and "I-Thou" distinction. Buber's theological perspective can be difficult to wade through, but if we take his main point, we have a tool to work with that may be useful especially as we look at our relationship to each other and to the Earth.

An "I-It" relationship is one characterized as our seeing the "other" as an object. All "Its" are simply objects to be manipulated, used and discarded when we are done with them. They are not connected to us in any way beyond their utility. (Far too often, we treat others in our lives as an "It" rather than relating to them as a "Thou".)

An "I-Thou" relationship treats the "Thou" as a meaningful encounter, one that is reciprocal. A "Thou" is not an object; it is a way of relating to another with respect, care, consideration, or love. As an example, the ultimate "Thou" is our relationship with the Divine; that relationship is sacred. On Earth, when we treat others, animals, plants, or the Earth itself as a "Thou", we acknowledge our intimate, connected, and personal relationship; they stop being an "It", an object, and become in relationship a "Thou"; they become integral to who we are.

Graham Hancock provides a concrete example regarding how this change in perspective matters. "It is not oil, or water, or mineral deposits, or food, or land, or any other economic resource that is truly scarce or precious or 'running out' in this bountiful earth of ours. What we are short of as a global species, what we seem reluctant to manifest, what we are failing to express and act out, is simply love, and in a way this should be the easiest problem in the world for us to solve – for it is within the capacity and the power of each and every one of us to give love if we choose to do so… The more power we have… the more it is our responsibility to love."[5] Again, we can easily move from an "I-It" to an "I-Thou" relationship. So simple, really.

In times past, the book *The Secret Lives of Plants* made a big hit; it seemed to resonate with thousands of readers and may well have caused most of us to wake up to the possibility that plants are more than they seem. Over time, much of the book was discredited by several studies, but in place of that, many scientists soldiered on with solid research on plants and now have much more concrete information to share with us about the world of plants. First, says Michael Pollan, "We must stop regarding plants as passive objects—the mute, immobile furniture of our world—and begin to treat them as protagonists in their own dramas, highly skilled in the ways of contending in nature."[6] Recall that Descartes, one of the founding fathers of contemporary science, insisted that only humans possessed self-consciousness. Animals could not suffer pain; their cries were mere reflexes and meaningless physiological noise. Today, of course, we know better, but could we be making the same mistake regarding our view of the life of plants? Before dismissing the possibility out of hand, let's look at the notions of intelligence and consciousness a bit more closely.

Intelligence and consciousness seem to be a property of life. Take bacteria, for example, "Bacteria colonies are seen to act like a unified intelligence."[7] Or as Michael Pollan notes, "Intelligence in plants resembles that exhibited in insect colonies, where it is thought to be an emergent property of a great many mindless individuals organized in a network. Much of the research on plant intelligence has been inspired by the new science of networks, distributed computing, and swarm behavior, which has demonstrated some of the ways in which remarkably brainy behavior can emerge in the absence of an actual brain." And if we take consciousness as a state of being awake and aware of one's environment, then perhaps plants do, in fact, have consciousness, although not a consciousness as we experience ours. We might consider plants as a "Thou" and "because plants are sensitive and intelligent beings, we are obliged to treat them with some degree of respect. That means protecting their habitats from destruction and avoiding practices such as genetic manipulation, growing plants in monocultures, and training them in bonsai."[8] Plants lack critical irreplaceable organs that animals have, and some plants are clearly identified as not edible or are poisonous, but others appear to have evolved to be eaten as part of their evolutionary strategy. They are part of a long chain of being in which light is consumed and then made available to the animal kingdom.

We will next look at a somewhat controversial and provocative view regarding how plants may communicate with humans.

The topic of psychedelics (synthetic) and entheogens (plant based hallucinogens) is fraught with difficulties. We have all heard horror stories of people who hurt themselves through the recreational misuse of these powerful drugs for hedonistic purposes. Here, the case for their value as aids in human understanding is presented as described by serious scientists, historians, and others who view the incredible possibilities latent in our exploration of these plants. Within this view is the perspective that we lost something precious when we discontinued using psychoactive plants. With so many people currently studying their relationship with *ayahuasca*, a plant entheogen, with shamans in South America, we may be on the threshold of rediscovery. At the very least, we would all benefit from a variety of controlled studies regarding the possible application of psychoactive plants to address ways we might extend our communication with the Earth and all that is beyond the pale of ordinary consciousness. We have kept the lid on any sort of controlled experimentation, extended research, and study of psychoactive plants far too long. In the words of Terrence McKenna, "The suppression of the natural human fascination with altered states of consciousness and the present perilous situation of all life on earth are intimately and causally connected. When we suppress access to shamanic ecstasy, we close off the refreshing waters of emotion that flow from having a deeply bonded, almost symbiotic relationship to the earth. As a consequence, the maladaptive social styles that encourage overpopulation, resource mismanagement, and environmental toxification develop and maintain themselves. No culture on earth is as heavily narcotized as the industrial West in terms of being inured to the consequences of maladaptive behavior. We pursue a business-as-usual attitude in a surreal atmosphere of mounting crises and irreconcilable contradictions." With that understanding in mind, let's proceed.

As it turns out, the history of entheogens has a lot to say about some aspects of contemporary life. For example, "A growing number of… scholars from many different countries… take the view that the first notions of the existence of supernatural realms and beings, the first "religious ideas about them, the first art representing them, and the first mythologies concerning them were all derived from the experiences of hallucinating shamans."[9] It is entirely conceivable that hallucinogens operating in the natural environment produce exopheromones, which may make possible a transfer of information from one species to another. It may be a way for plants to communicate directly with humans.

In the nineteenth century, educated people had to come to terms with the Darwin's theory, which argued that we evolved from apes. As Terrence McKenna reminds us, "We must now come to terms with the fact that those apes were stoned apes. Being stoned seems to have been our unique characteristic."

It may well be that the hallucinogens around 100,000 years ago improved our ability to process information, acted as a promoter of creative imagination, revealed our spiritual nature, assisted in the creation of language and fostered an increased sense of conscious self-awareness…The ingestion of mushrooms appears to have helped "religious ritual, calendar making, and natural magic [to] come into their own."[10]

The eating of a particular sort of mushroom in Late Paleolithic times suggests humans developed in ways not otherwise demonstrable. "Psilocybin's main synergistic effect seems ultimately to be in the domain of language. It excites vocalization; it empowers articulation; it transmutes language into something that is visibly beheld. It could have had an impact on the sudden emergence of consciousness and language use in early humans. We literally may have eaten our way to higher consciousness."[11] We need to remember that the ingestion of entheogens speeds up processes that are already present in living entities; they amplify what is already latent within. Entheogens do not cause consciousness; consciousness is present in some degree in all forms of life. We came by the desire to ingest entheogens with other common ancestors that also ate psychoactive plants. The attraction to hallucinogenic plants was not limited to humans. "Scientists have established that the ability to hallucinate… is shared by other mammals and also by birds, bees, butterflies, ants and spiders, many of which are known actively to seek out psychoactive substances."[12] It appears that the domestication of wild cattle spurred interspecies codependency because a particular mushroom grows only in cattle dung. It might be suggested that the growth of mushrooms was one of the first crops humans regularly harvested. In this connection, perhaps our western conception of Christmas is illustrative of how psychedelic use has affected our mythology of Santa and flying reindeer.

The story of Santa and his reindeer may well have come from a remote North Pole Siberian indigenous tribe who herded reindeer. It was likely that one of their shaman discovered the odd behavior of reindeer that ate red Fly Agaric (aka: *Amanita muscaria*), mushrooms growing under specific evergreen trees. The shaman watched the reindeer drink their own urine. The shaman copied the reindeer, that is, drank the urine, and had a psychedelic experience. Later, he and the tribe picked the red mushrooms and dried them on the branches as they hunted for more mushrooms; later he would gather them in a large sack, stuff them in stockings, bring them home and hang the now-filled stockings by the fire.

Flying to other worlds to gain insight into how to help others is a common shamanic experience; it is how they bring back gifts of healing from the other world. One of the effects of ingesting these mushrooms is the drastic distortion of space and time; it is common to feel as if oneself and reindeer are flying. As Matt Toussaint, the author of *Shaman Claus: The Shamanic Origins of Christmas* notes, "The shaman's journey and return was ultra-important to the survival of the whole community. What they brought back with them was often a matter of life and death… they would learn knowledge and wisdom directly from the sacred plants, their journeys, and from the spirits they interacted with."

Often during the winter solstice, the tribal members would erect a symbolic sacred tree, the very same tree where the mushrooms grew, in their yurts. There was a hole/chimney for the smoke from the central fire to let out the smoke -- and facilitate their spirit's connection with other worlds. In one of their three worlds, the North Star sat above the world tree erected in the yurt.

Matt Toussaint notes, "The sacred Amanita with its red, golden and orange coloring as well as its capacity to offer direct experience and connection with divinity was also regarded as a symbol for the Sun and its life-giving and saving properties. The Sun – or the Son – is the savior, born on the 25th of December as the bringer of light, harbinger and liberator of life on Earth."

Sometimes the perception is that to ingest an entheogen is to choose to escape from ordinary reality; however, for those who study the effects on human consciousness, it is quite the opposite. As Gregory Sams notes, "The psychedelic experience in not embraced as an escape from our world but as a ticket to escape from the single channel; to see the bigger picture and the smaller picture; to see our world from a different perspective, even from a different dimension." To get the maximum benefit from ingesting any hallucinogen, one has to be intellectually, psychologically, and emotionally prepared. As a case in point, Francis Harry Compton Crick, one of the Nobel Prize co-winners in 1962, won the prize for presenting the structure of the DNA-helix, the molecule that carries genetic information from one generation to the other. He used LSD in several sessions to boost his mental powers. That was a time when LSD was still legal. Psychoactive plants reliably and repeatedly appear to open the valves that the brain normally uses to limit what we experience.[13] Entheogens may tune us in to wavelengths not normally available to the human brain in ordinary states of consciousness. As McKenna observed among shamans, "The mystery of our own consciousness and powers of self-reflection is somehow linked to this channel of communication, the unseen mind that shamans insist is the spirit of the living world of nature. For shamans and shamanic cultures, exploration of this mystery has always been a credible alternative to living in a confining materialist culture."

The power and influence of ancient Greek thought in Western culture is without question one of the most significant in our history. We continue to be inspired by their wisdom, poetry, and philosophy. What is not generally known is that virtually anybody who was anybody in Greek culture – and that included Plato and Socrates -- spent time at Eleusis, where, with direction, support, and guidance, they imbibed what we now know was a psychoactive plant. Writes McKenna, "There is little doubt that at Eleusis something was drunk by each initiate and each saw something during the initiation that was utterly unexpected, transformative, and capable of remaining with each participant as a powerful memory for the rest of their life. It is an incredible testament to the obtuseness of the scholar of the dominator society that not until 1964 did someone make bold to suggest that a hallucinogenic plant must have been involved." It is hard to imagine many in our contemporary world willing to learn the nature of anything from psychoactive plants. However, if they did engage with such an experience under controlled conditions, they might "learn the degree to which unexamined cultural values and limitation of language have made us the unwitting prisoners of our own assumptions. For it cannot be without reason that wherever in the world hallucinogenic indoles have been utilized, their use has been equated with magical self-healing and regeneration. The low incidence of serious mental illness among such population is well documented."[14] Could there be a safe, therapeutic environment created where all the people who are considered leaders might go to receive the same sort of knowledge granted to the early Greeks?

Now, it is not necessary for everyone to engage with entheogens. It may be quite helpful to the rest of us if those who do are willing to learn, share and teach the rest of us what the plant world may choose to tell us. Such teaching may help all of us survive and thrive harmoniously. Even if most of us don't want to engage with plants on an experiential level, all of us can choose to be aware, connected, and respectful of all other forms of life. We can act toward others and the Earth as a "Thou." We can shift to a deeper level of relating. New possibilities await such a transformation.

Fresh Perspective endnotes

1. Suzuki, David, " Reflections of an Eco-Warrior", *Zoomer*, Dec 2017/ Jan 2018, PP. 78-79.

2. Goldstein, Rebecca, Plato at The Googleplex: Why Philosophy Won't Go Away (2014), Pantheon Books, NY, p. 14.

3. McKenna, Terence, Food of the Gods: The Search For the Original Tree of Knowledge (1992), Bantam Books, NY, p. 179.

4. McKenna, Dennis J., Reflections In A Rear-View Mirror: Speculations On Novelty Theory and The End Times in Hancock, Graham, Magicians Of The Gods (2015), Coronet Pub, UK, p. 50.

5. Hancock, 2015, pp. 284 & 286.

6. Pollan, Michael, The Intelligent Plant, The New Yorker, December 23, 2013.

7. Sams, Gregory, Stellar Consciousness, in Hancock, 2015, p. 37.

8. Pollan, 2003.

9. Hancock, 2005, p. 35

10. McKenna, 1992, pp. 20 & 24.

11. McKenna, 1992, p. 42.

12. Hancock, 2005, pp. 578-579.

13. McKenna, 1992, pp. 50-51.

14. McKenna, 1992, p. 229

2

The Beginning

In the early days of movies, the plot of several comedies involved two goofy characters, Stan and Oliver, who got into trouble repeatedly. One line of dialogue became classic. Whenever Stan would get Oliver into some kind of trouble (which was a lot), he would tell his long-time friend, "Well, here's another nice mess you've gotten me into!" Perhaps that line was prophetic of western culture's current state of affairs.

Before getting to the list of our problems, let's take a step back to see if we can shed some light on how we got to this dire set of circumstances. As is usually the case, our current malaise has a history.

Virtually every issue afflicting human beings starts with the notion of separation, a condition built so completely into our unconscious worldview that most of us don't even see it. But it's there. It can be seen in the religious sense when there is talk about being separate from God or Spirit; or in an ecological sense when there is talk about being separate from Nature; or when there is talk about being separate from community or the Other; or when psychologists talk about being separate from our authentic selves; or when we treat illness in the body as separate from the mind.

The very concept or idea of separation may need some clarification. Let's start with birth. When a person is born, she is unique, separate, and dependent upon the mother. She is born into this world both as a separate individual yet is one who has needs that can only be satisfied as an utterly dependent connected being. In fact the two states of existence are inseparable. The satisfaction of the needs of the individual will always be connected to some other person or persons throughout life. Not only that, each of us has needs that can only be provided from our environment -- think food, clothing, shelter, and so on. Add to that, consider our necessary connection to the larger community, which provides all the items we use everyday, and it becomes clear that individuals cannot live without being connected throughout their lives. Although we are unique and separate beings, we live in a connected world from birth to death. To insist on our being only separate, to ignore our connection to Nature, to ignore these fundamental facts of our existence is to court disaster, which is arguably our current condition as a civilization.

It may be said that we are who we are because of our connection with everything outside of ourselves. As humans, we intrinsically need to belong, to connect, to merge with others, to collaborate, to partner with others. We are long past the view that a life of competition, isolation, atomization, and alienation lead to a healthy life. That view is, at bottom, the prime cause of much of what is destroying our lives and the planet itself. The time has come to correct this false view and reclaim our humanity. For example, there is overwhelming evidence that people who are self-absorbed, cynical and hostile to the world are more likely to have a heart attack. Those who are socially isolated are in the neighborhood of three times more likely to die of a heart attack compared to others who feel connected to others. (Even connecting with a pet increases the odds of living longer.) When there is an emphasis on individualism in a social system, the measures of health, urban safety, and a host of other indices reflecting life satisfaction fall dramatically. As Lynne McTaggart, in *The Bond* notes, "Shooting each other is simply the most extreme version of the kind of relationships you and I engage in when we act against nature and communicate from a selfish, competitive point of view."

Let's explore and extend our understanding of the reality that we are part of something much larger than the more mundane world of ordinary existence. We know, for example, there are gravitational and other forces at work that keep all the planets in regular orbits around the sun. We know that the Earth is one of the planets in the solar system and that our sun, about 93 million miles away, determines much of the condition of our life on Earth. We know we are subject to the natural laws that govern everything from what happens in outer space to what happens in the smallest particles or photons of light that make up matter. What may not be as clear is the degree to which we are affected by the cosmos. There is compelling evidence that our physical size, longevity, mental stability, our aggressive inclinations, and even our motivation may be conditioned by this cosmos. Somehow, there is a force that connects "all that is" to our unique sense of self. In short, biology and behavior resonate with what is happening in the cosmos. What seems like unique individual behavior is, in fact, connected to a much larger entity, the cosmos.

For example, when there is an increase in geomagnetic activity, (the Earth's magnetic field) blood gets thicker, heart attacks are more common, death from cardiovascular issues increases. In addition, electrical activity in the brain gets fuzzy during magnetic storms. Moods are subject to wild swings. Risky behavior increases. Who hasn't heard of the increase in the number of general mental health issues during the full and new moon phases? When the moon is in full or is new, there are more attempted suicides, epileptic seizures, and incidents of sudden infant death syndrome. During the greater solar activity in our sun, the birth size of children is larger.

Reports of increased acts of terrorism often match the cycle of the Earth's geomagnetic index. When the increase in mass violence was correlated with the Russian Revolution, Stalin was so put out with the idea that there was more to the Communist Revolution than ideology, he imprisoned in the Siberian gulag the scientist who discovered the correlation.

The desire to merge with another comes with birth. The infant's brain's first impulse is to merge with the brain of mom. The desire to merge continues throughout life. For example, whenever we want to connect with another person, the first impulse of both of our brains is to copy each other. This is what is called "entraining the brain" and is what happens when, for example, a healer sends out energy to one seeking healing. Touching others with appreciation and kindness will often entrain both yours and the other person's brain waves. Again, from McTaggart, "Individual living things absorb the light emitted from each other and send back wave-interference patterns, as though they are having a conversation. Once the light waves of one organism are absorbed by another organism, the first organism's light begins trading information in synchrony… With every waking moment, we are taking in something else's light." It may be said that is how we understand others, how we make sense of the multiplicity of sensations continuously coming toward us: we imagine other's experience as if it were our own. We have mirror neurons, that is, we have sections of our brain that set in motion the full range of emotions we observe in another person. It is as if we, too, are experiencing the same experience as the other. We do this often just by seeing a facial expression or observing body language. This is how we understand another person. To quote from *The Bond* once again, "Mirror neurons are meant to work out not only what someone is doing and how he feels about it, but also why he is doing it… The neurons do not fire if the goal of the action is unclear… Perceiving the world is not an individual affair, limited to our own mental capacities, but a process involving shared neural circuitry. We internalize the experience of others at every moment, automatically and immediately, without conscious effort, using a neural shorthand created of our own experience. In the very act of connecting with someone, even on the most superficial level, we are involved in a relationship of the utmost intimacy. Our understanding of the complexities of our world occurs through the constant melding of the observer with the observed." To engage our mirror neurons is to acknowledge that we --at some fundamental level -- want to agree with each other.

There is ample evidence that we are wired to be compassionate, to help others, to be altruistic, to connect. Contrary to much popular opinion, selfishness is essentially culturally conditioned; it is not a natural human trait. Caring about others is automatic and basic to our biology. As McTaggart notes, "As a good deal of evidence shows, helping not only feels good; it also promotes health and even longevity. It may even be an essential component of the contented life."

In fact, we can even be affected by others at a remote level and not even realize it is happening. Take our social world, for example, without realizing how connected we are, we choose our mates, the support groups and clubs we like, the people we trust to give us advice, and so on. We prefer the company of others who have similar demographics, personal characteristics, interests and behaviors. In fact, there is some evidence that suicide bombers have a deep-seated need to be accepted by their group and are less motivated by religious ideology per se. It has been said that, "People don't simply kill and die for a cause… They kill and die for each other." A notion worth exploring with a combat veteran. Friends and colleagues matter more for most of us than our relatives.

Our experience of separation brings bad and good news. The bad news is that we experience our lives as separate from others and the world; the good news is that we experience our lives as separate from others and the world. However, it is our inherent longing from birth for connection, for bonding, for coherence that makes us human and capable of managing and transcending our separation; we long for union. But first we have to acknowledge our initial condition of separateness and how our felt lack of connection has contaminated our lives.

It is not a large leap to see how in western culture, Nature is one of those objects we see as something we control and dominate for the benefit of the self. Science and technology have given us tremendous benefits and have also become the primary tools for this control and dominance. We use technology to distance ourselves from nature's rhythms, from the physical reality that surrounds us. Most of us condition our lives around the schedules of machines rather than relating to natural rhythms. Consider the fact that we ship unseasonal food across the planet all year long, that we use air-conditioning to buttress our vulnerability to heat, that we fly or sail in hours where it once took days to travel, or that we communicate planet-wide with a push of a few buttons. In all these cases we rise well beyond natural limitations. In principle as long as we act within known abilities, we can ignore Nature at will. As Charles Eisenstein writes, "The more we dominate, own, and control, the more separate we experience ourselves. The more separate we experience ourselves, the greater the urge to dominate, to own, to control."[1] The loop is self-reinforcing.

With the advent of modern scientific thinking with its dictum that the role of the scientist is to strip nature bare to reveal its secrets, we took the notion of separation to a new level. The detached observer is the very model of the separate being. Nature is an object that may be controlled, dominated, and manipulated to whatever ends we determine. Nature is simply an external object, having no human connection beyond utility. It seems as if every advance in technology further distances us from Nature. The dominance of the idea of our separation from the world was further reinforced with the influence of Newton and Darwin, a topic addressed in more detail in another chapter. As Lynn McTaggart noted, "Our current scientific story is more than three hundred years old, largely based on the discoveries of Isaac Newton, who described a universe in which all matter was separate and operated according to fixed laws in time and space... The worldview arising form these discoveries was bolstered by the philosophical implications of Charles Darwin's theory of evolution, with its suggestion that survival is available only to the robust individual. These, in essence, are stories that idealize a competitive type of separateness. From the moment we are born, we are told that for every winner there must be a loser. From that constricted vision we have fashioned our world."[2] (We will get to some of the consequences of that view in good time.) Science, in this view, reflects one aspect of the old Manichean conception of dualism, which is the idea that virtually everything is divided into two separate parts; matter and spirit; human and other; inert and alive; body and mind; the list actually is quite long, but the idea is clear. Idealization of our separateness has removed us so completely from Nature that we now see ourselves as lords of the universe, totally dominant, virtually invincible. For many, there is nothing that a detached scientific enterprise cannot solve or create.

As Nature is separate, so is God, who resides in the heavens disconnected from us. Or more likely, God is non-existent; she does not even exist. Science and technology have extended our sense of separation from the cosmos. As Joseph Needleman writes in *An Unknown World*, "The general worldview of modernity rejects the existence of higher levels of being, higher levels of reality which are invisible to the sense-based knowledge offered by science." We, and all we observe, are simply matter in one form or another.

At some point, a person has to ask, "How did we ever get so lost, so divorced from reality?" And again, we have to go back in history to find, if not the root, certainly a significant cause of our current malaise. But first, any argument for the diagnosis and possible solution of the problem of contemporary civilization needs to be stated at the outset. Neal Donald Walsh, in *The Overhaul of Humanity*, lays out the problem in explicit terms.

"We begin with a hypothesis:

The world is not the way we wish it were. Life on our planet is not the way we want it to be.

A question:

How is it possible for seven billion human beings to all desire the same thing (peace, security, opportunity, prosperity, happiness, and love) and to be unable to collectively produce it... even after trying for thousands of years?

Conclusion:

There is something we do not fully understand about life, and understanding of which would change everything."

Let's see if we can move our understanding of life a bit and perhaps come closer to recognizing the elusive cause of the problem.

This matter of causes of the malaise of our time has many perspectives. What follows is just one of many equally valid arguments. When humans discovered agriculture and moved away from being hunter-gatherers, their whole way of being, of existing, changed profoundly. For now, let's simply note that the agricultural revolution that occurred somewhere around 8,000 to 12,000 years ago is still reverberating in the twenty first century.

The agricultural revolution may be the most important and significant event in human history. It followed the end of the last ice age. Climate change, which may have been exacerbated by a series of comet collisions with the earth, and/or the eruption of several major volcanoes could have been the major cause of the change from living as hunter-gatherers to farmers. No other climatic development has had such a radical, transformative effect on how we think of ourselves, other animals, our relationship to Nature, our conception of religion and political organization. We have not yet recovered from the effects of the agricultural revolution that followed from the end of the last ice age.

Historical records from that period are scant; hunter-gatherers had an oral culture and largely because of that, there was no written language, no history. They left few artifacts. Archeologists must piece together what little information there is from excavated ancient sites. Anthropologists have studied the culture of contemporary indigenous hunter-gatherers to gain some insight into how they manage foraging in the forests and to infer how ancient peoples who had comparable ways of existing might have lived under similar conditions. Climatologists, zoologists, botanists and geologists can tell us some things about the climate of ancient time and the likely accessibility of game and plants available to peoples long gone. But a large part of what we now think about these ancient cultures is a patchwork of guesswork with reasonable approximations of probability tossed in the mix. Of course, many theories abound, some more outrageous than others. This discussion conveys the more-or-less conventional view.

In contrast, we know quite a lot about the early agricultural communities and how they differed from the hunter-gatherers. There are some archaic records, some version of language that can be deciphered, and many visible and excavated archeological sites. In addition, archeologists, climatologists, zoologists, botanists and geologists among others, have brought their expertise to the study of these ancient agriculturally based ruins and have been able to tell the rest of us some of what developed at that time.

Given these caveats, let us begin to contrast the difference in organized living arrangements, psychology, spirituality, and consciousness between hunter-gatherers and the early agriculturalists. More importantly we need to remember that we humans have been hunter-gatherers for well over 100,000 years and agriculturalists for a mere 10,000 years. No doubt, all those thousands of years of existence before agriculture have planted something indelible into our brains and bodies that have a more or less permanent effect on how we experience the world. As Paul Shepard noted in *Coming Home to the Pleistocene*, "The transformation from hunter/gatherer to agrarian economies took place over the past twelve thousand years. This length of time is insignificant in terms of geological history – or, for that matter, in terms of human history that began with the appearance of Homo sapiens some four hundred thousand years ago, our genus, Homo, at two million years, and our family, *Hominidae*, six million years ago."

There is a tendency among some people when looking at a bygone time to see it as some idealized Eden, a time when the things that worry us were not in existence. The reality – insofar as we can tell -- was that primitive peoples were sophisticated in how their tribes were constructed. They recognized, for example, "that power is plural, societies are egalitarian, and leadership is not monopolized but changing and dispersed."[3] (Imagine for a moment that this conception was true in our time!) They lived under environmentally harsh conditions (Perhaps the least of which is to imagine what it would be like to live with no bug spray in the wilderness!), often endured severe weather, occasionally experienced conflict with other clans, were subject to disease, had no time for leisurely extended political, spiritual, or philosophical discussions, and likely had short lives. It is apparent, however, that they did not attempt to master Nature. They were connected viscerally to it and, as much by default as otherwise, they lived in harmony with it.

Theirs was an oral culture, where not only humans but everything could speak. The hunter-gatherers likely experienced space and place intuitively. From what we can tell from the study of current indigenous peoples, specific spaces have specific powers and people have to negotiate their relationship with those places. In short, places were not symbolic abstractions, but rather real environments that called for specific behaviors. As David Abram noted, "Nonhuman animals, plants and even 'inanimate' rivers once spoke to our tribal ancestors." A person had to experience places to know their power and to know how to respond because, as often as not, there may have been more than one sacred aspect in a place. For ancient peoples all that existed had spirit, a particular energy, sentience, sacredness. Such spaces were not always visibly beautiful, but they were channels for communication with spiritual entities. These days, we diminish that sensibility by calling it animism, a primitive form of religion. But to do so is to diminish our capacity to connect with our environment. For it is well to remember, as James Swan writes in Sacred Places "Each of us descended from people who worshipped nature, and the symbols, forms, and energies of our ancestors reside somewhere in our personal unconscious as well as our collective unconscious, waiting for us to tap them and awaken human resources to renew our primal roots of well-being."

The respect of hunter-gathers extended beyond space and place to include animals that were more than mere objects to serve human ends. Animals had purposes of their own; they did not exist only to serve humans. Animals had special access to wisdom. Animals could be bearers of messages from a sacred domain. "Traditional wise people say that if you want to know the truth you should go talk to the animal for they are the cleanest source of knowledge."[4] (Four legged and flying animals are best). And yet, animals were a source of food, too. The killing of animals was usually enshrouded in a respectful ritual, one that acknowledged a life given to humans was a gift to be honored.

The agricultural revolution brought us many benefits: it freed up some members of the community from having to till the soil and allowed for the diversification of roles we take for granted today. It made civilization as we know it possible. As we will see, the transformation was not all about the benefits of farming. As Ronald Wright observed in *A Short History of Progress*, "The invention of agriculture is itself a runaway train, leading to vastly expanded population but seldom solving the food problem because of two inevitable (or nearly inevitable) consequences. The first is biological: the population grows until it hits the bounds of the food supply. The second is social: all civilizations become hierarchical; the upward concentration of wealth ensures that there can never be enough to go around."

The problem of the shortage of food can be ameliorated to some degree for a period of time by increasing technological fixes, but even technology won't work after a while. Societies keep getting more complex, outrunning the system's capacity to develop the necessary technology to solve the problem. We see this issue in our time. Perhaps Paul Shepard makes too harsh a point when he notes, "If there is a single complex of events responsible for the deterioration of human health and ecology, agricultural civilization is it. At its worst, agriculture is industrial and corporate, poisoning the whole planet with chemical compounds not found in nature."[6]

In contrast, the world of the hunter gatherer is instructive. Let's take the observation of David Abram in *The Spell of the Sensuous*, when he commented on the Americas before the invasion of Europeans, "That indigenous peoples can have gathered, hunted, fished, and settled these lands for such a tremendous span of time without severely degrading the continent's wild integrity readily confounds the notion that humans are innately bound to ravage their earthly surroundings."

Theorists generally think that agriculture was not a sudden invention. Because of climate change, many of the huge animals -- the elk, reindeer, horse, and great auroch (an elephant sized cow) -- hunted for food were long since gone. There was a significant learning curve to adjust to the new reality. Cultivating sufficient crops to feed the newly emergent civilizations who began to live in settlements evolved over something like five thousand years. In these early years of farming, there was a shift from looking at Nature as a Thou, that is, as a living presence to be accorded reverence, to one of seeing Nature as a Thing, something that exists apart from the works of man to be manipulated to produce consumable goods. The psychology seems to have gone from one of living by chance or circumstance to one of conscious manipulation of the environment; to have gone from the sense of grace and gifts freely offered by Nature to bartering with the elements for control of the outcome, a sustainable crop. In short, humans went from finding to making, from receiving to negotiating, from transient camps to the fixed shelters of the village.[7]

Animals once seen as having sapience and intelligence as well as purposes of their own lost their mystical ancestry with humans. Plants were no longer part of a shared home; instead, to the degree it was possible, animals (and plants) were domesticated and controlled as humans determined to have more and more power. Animals were hitched to machines like the grindstone and water pumps. From there it was a short step from the ownership and control of animals to the ownership and control of others. Slavery only came into existence with agriculture. As Guy Murchie writes in *The Seven Mysteries of Life,* "The evidence shows it was only with settled living and civilization that owning slaves and other property became feasible. And this explains why human slavery evolved so gradually, along with agriculture, villages, animal domestication and particularly the invention of war, which after all, is what provided the prisoners who became the first slaves."

Man became lord and master and controller of all. As Shepard noted, "Domestication changed means of production, altered social relationships, and increased environmental destruction… From ecosystems at dynamic equilibrium ten thousand years ago the farmers created subsystems with pests and weeds by the time of the first walled towns five thousand years ago."[8]

Animals and others were either part of the community in the village and held value or were not; either things were wild or tame, good plants or weeds, useful things or the worthless objects of Nature. A man worked for tomorrow – that's when the crops could be harvested -- and diminished the value of foraging for food today. "The angry God that arose in early civilization is also linked to the concept of good and evil and the concept of sin. The corn is good, the weeds are bad. The bees are good, the locusts bad. The sheep are good, the wolves bad."[9] It wasn't much of a step from animals to make some people bad and some good.

Reaping what you sow (An agricultural phrase, borne of the time) became the norm. The reality that one could reap what was not sown because Nature was typically generous was cast aside. The present became slave to the future; today's labor brings tomorrow's harvest.[10] As man increasingly valued what was made or created, he began to internalize the notion that he himself was made and what he created himself to be became his highest value. He was no longer a part of nature, but separate from it. As Charles Eisenstein noted, "Agriculture inaugurated our conception of the earth as a resource or asset, defined primarily by its productivity. The land gradually lost its intrinsic value – its sacredness – and assumed an extrinsic, conditional value based on what it could produce. For the first time there was good land and bad land." In brief, the concept of duality or good things-in-opposition-to-bad things became the norm. A norm that is now so endemic in our thinking we are barely aware of the dualism created so long ago.

The many changes in thinking that came with agriculture didn't come without liabilities. Now there was the possibility of a bad crop, or the invasion of pests, which meant the possibility of the scarcity of food. Security replaced the intimacy and sharing of the forager as hoarding issues became commonplace. Now there were others who might take one's possessions. Weapons had to be created to fend off intruders and thieves. Frequent wars became the new reality. The sheer daily drudgery of working the land everyday replaced the twenty or so hours a week the hunter-gatherer spent getting food. Gone was the fact that Nature provided what was needed. "Domestication would create a catastrophic biology of nutritional deficiencies, alternating feast and famine, health and epidemic, peace and social conflict all set in millennial rhythms of slowly collapsing ecosystems."[11]

Gone too, was the sacredness of Nature. "Agriculture lent itself to imagining gods in the image of humankind who controlled humans as they controlled domesticated nature and as men controlled women."[12] The gods became supernatural – as opposed to natural – beings. The sky gods repudiated natural entities who called Earth home. Temples replaced sacred spaces. As Charles Eisenstein observed, "It is no coincidence that the abstraction of spirit from matter, the removal of the abode of the gods into a heavenly realm and the emergence of patriarchy all happened at about the same time."

The process was so total we don't even see it today, but the effects are everywhere. As Paul Shepard notes, "Everywhere that 'world' religions – Judaism, Christianity, Buddhism, and Islam – have gone, earth shrines, sacred forests, springs, and other places with their wild inhabitants have vanished, replaced often with temples or churches." Giving offerings to the gods was instituted with the advent of agriculture; it did not exist among hunter-gatherers.[25]

The earlier religions tended to be theocratic. They enslaved rather than liberated the peoples of the time. (Virtually none of the major religions value life on Earth; all rewards are in some location skyward.) Since monotheism placed god in the heavens and desacralized all forms of life on Earth, it diminished the inherent spirit of all forms of life because as lower beings, they had no spirit; this eventually included other humans who had other, false gods.[13]

In matters of social organization, the agricultural revolution significantly altered human relations. Shepard notes the differences, "All people instinctively differentiate among themselves socially. But cultures differ in their criteria for doing so. Among hunter/gatherers the criteria tend to be age, gender, and ability; in complex societies the social distinctions are more often wealth, power, and kingship." Males dominate as chiefs or leaders in almost all cases among agricultural communities. This may explain to some degree why most leaders are males in contemporary times. They have inherited a legacy from the past. Historically, such a concentration of power in the few creates problems for the many. "The concentration of power at the top of large-scale societies gives the elite a vested interest in the status quo; they continue to prosper in darkening times long after the environment and general populace begin to suffer."[14]

Perhaps the most damming criticism of the fruits of agriculture comes from an organization called Dark Mountain. In their view, we are "highly evolved apes with an array of talents and abilities which we are unleashing without sufficient thought, control, compassion or intelligence. Apes who have constructed a sophisticated myth of their own importance with which to sustain their civilizing project. Apes whose project has been to tame, to control, to subdue or to destroy — to civilize the forests, the deserts, the wild lands and the seas, to impose bonds on the minds of their own in order that they might feel nothing when they exploit or destroy their fellow creatures. "[15] While this view is stark, a more moderate view, as quoted by Paul Shepard, may be more palatable. "Physiologist Rene Dubos observes that humans can adapt (via culture) to 'starless skies, treeless avenues, shapeless buildings, tasteless bread, joyless celebrations, spiritless pleasures – to a life without reverence for the past, love for the present, or poetical anticipations of the future.' But, he says,' it is questionable that a man can retain his physical and mental health if he loses contact with the natural forces that have shaped his biological and mental nature."

We have continued to divorce our lives from our connection with Nature at our own peril. Just how that peril is manifesting currently is the topic of the next chapter.

Beginning endnotes

1.   Eisenstein, <u>The Ascent of Humanity: Civilization and the Human Sense of Self</u> (2007), Evolver Editions, North Atlantic Books, Berkeley, CA, p. 168.

2.   Our New Story: Recognizing the Bond, Lynne McTaggart, in Hubbard, 2012, p. 183.

3.   Abram, David, <u>The Spell of the Sensuous: Perception and Language in a More-Than-Human World</u> (1997), Vintage Books, NY, p. 131.

4.   Shepard, Paul, <u>Nature and Madness</u> (1998), University of Georgia Press, Athens, GE, p. 94.

5.   Shepard, Paul, <u>Coming Home to the Pleistocene</u> (1998), Edited by Florence R. Shepard, Island Press/Shearwater books, Covelo, CA, p. 82.

6.   Shepard, 1998, p.19.

7.   Shepard, 1998, p. 81.

8.   Shepard, 1998, p. 82

9.   Eisenstein, Charles, <u>The Ascent of Humanity: Civilization and the Human Sense of Self</u> (2007), Evolver Editions, North Atlantic Books, Berkeley, CA, p. 85.

10.   Eisenstein, 2007, p. 71.

11.   Shepard, Paul, <u>Nature and Madness</u> (1998), University of Georgia Press, Athens, GE, p. 83

12.   Shepard, 1998, p. 96.

13.   Shepard, 1998, p. 123.

14.   Wright, Ronald, <u>A Short History of Progress</u> (2004), House of Anansi Press Inc., Toronto, Ontario, Canada, p. 109.

15.   Dark Mountain Project, http://dark-mountain.net/about/manifesto/

3

Resource Extraction

American culture is in big trouble. We live in a time
of crisis, a crisis at several levels as anyone who has been
paying attention can attest. The specifics are everywhere and
abundant. Some details: The financial system appears rigged
to favor the wealthiest citizens at the expense of everyone
else, the political system is regularly gridlocked, and the
educational system is overburdened. We have a more or less
permanent underclass. We are on a permanent war footing,
borrowing money that cannot be repaid to fund an expanding
military empire. Any number of species are becoming
irretrievably extinct. Natural resources are being depleted at
an unsustainable rate leading to the eventual collapse of
current society as we know it. Soon poisoned air and water
will gravitate beyond contaminated cities like New Delhi to
infect the rest of the world's urban civilizations. We are
increasingly ignoring the old, if vulgar aphorism, "Don't shit
where you eat."

Naomi Klein, in This Changes Everything, outlines
the main issue of our time. She writes, "We tell ourselves all
kinds of … implausible no-consequences stories all the time,

about how we can ravage the world and suffer no adverse effects... We extract and do not replenish and wonder why the fish have disappeared and the soil requires ever more 'inputs' (like phosphate) to stay fertile. We occupy countries and arm their militias and then wonder why they hate us. We drive down wages, ship jobs overseas, destroy worker protections, hollow out local economies, then wonder why people can't afford to shop as much as they used to. We offer those failed shoppers subprime mortgages instead of steady jobs and then wonder why no one foresaw that a system built on bad debts would collapse."

For many of us, the pressing issues of climate change, immigration, fossil fuel dependence, and all the other ecological concerns easily slip into the abstract as we go about our busy lives. Many of us do what we can: recycle, diminish energy use, buy local, and so on. What I'd like to do now is focus a bit of light on these difficult matters, which tend to be and stay invisible because looking at them in terms of their human cost is so painful, and so much money is spent on preventing our seeing the true cost of the ecological destruction so prevalent in our time. Let me be explicit. The Western world's dependence on fossil fuels and resource extraction is costing lots of people their lives. If this sounds overly dramatic, let's pause and take a look at the evidence.

But first, here is a question to think about. If you were promised a million dollars to kill a nameless South American Indian and never, ever be caught, would you do it? (We will come back to this question and some answers further on.)

The history of colonialism is well documented in books available in any decent library or bookstore. I'm not about to recapitulate all the horrors of what happened in detail but will say only that in the early days of Western imperial colonialism, countries like England, France, Belgium, Germany, Holland, (and later, the US) went to Africa, South America, the Caribbean and other remote geographic locations and simply set up a temporary government and took resources they wanted after either killing or enslaving the local population. (The colonial process is still going on, of course, but the way it manifests has changed.) All the extracted resources went to the mother country where fortunes were (and are) made. When the resources were gone, the western power in place simply left the colonized country in skeletal condition, the people in complete disarray in every significant way. Few ordinary citizens in the western countries were aware of the process of extraction or the cost in human lives for the bounty they were enjoying.

Today, there are still huge reserves of oil, mineral, and other resources in the ground and in the ocean. The problem is that most of the high-demand resources like oil and rare minerals have already been extracted from the easy-access locations. Today, they are harder to get and more expensive to extract. Still, resource extraction proceeds with alarming success because contemporary western civilization requires huge quantities of resources to maintain and sustain industrial production to support our way of life.

In the past, when an oil company or mining outfit extracted resources, they dealt with the elites in the country to gain access, paid whatever royalties to the government in power (usually quite corrupt and easily bribed) and began operation. What is known is that the western company went into the remote regions where the resource to be extracted was often located, removed the local indigenous peoples to urban slums, took their property, destroyed their villages, polluted the water with toxic chemicals, and laid waste to the natural environment. They created a wasteland. (A quick example: the Canadian tar sands). The process continues to this day. Because the extraction process is largely hidden, and because these companies have huge budgets, public relations firms who create their worldly image, and technical approval from the corrupt government officials, they easily get away with what amounts to the willful destruction of our fellow human beings, their communities, and the natural environment. Again the question is pertinent, "If you could get a million dollars and never be found out, would you kill a nameless South American Indian?" Multi-national corporations usually answer the question in the affirmative. And the rest of us are complicit as well as we go about consuming virtually all of the resources extracted so brutally from largely remote jungles or oceans often displacing indigenous peoples. We are in effect, if not in a direct literal sense, still behaving in a way through our consumerism that leads to approving of the killing of that nameless South American Indian.

To review briefly what was discussed in a previous chapter: For thousands and thousands of years, humankind had lived in harmony with nature – sometimes with difficulty -- drawing sustenance, meaning, and understanding from the starry heavens above to the earth we walk upon. The universe and all other living things had their own purposes, had a presence; we and they were connected. From time-to-time, prophets, outspoken critics of society, and mystics reminded us that we were not the crown of creation; we were only one part of the whole, not the whole itself. They told us there was (and is) something greater than the fabulous human ego, narrow human purpose, and self-aggrandizing human accomplishment. Historically, these observations have been regularly ignored. Being the creative beings we are, new techniques were developed to further our disconnection from Nature until the prevailing view became what it is now: Nature is inert, has no purpose beyond what we ascribe to it. We live in a soulless, meaningless universe and because we exist in such a world, we too have a soulless and meaningless life.

It is a pretty grim picture. Nothing is sacred beyond our ego's needs and desires. As Francis Weller in *The Wild Edge of Sorrow* notes more poetically, "We have all but forgotten the intimate connection between our breath and the trees, flowering plants, and oceans that offer us their gift of oxygen. We could not exist without this luscious world surrounding our senses with beauty and delight. We would indeed 'die of a great loneliness' without the others with whom we share this animate earth."

This loss of that connection has led to the fiction of believing in materialism as a foundation upon which to build a life. The major institutions of society– science, religion, education, public policy –- are bereft of any sense of sacredness, awe, and mystery. They have fostered a sense of alienation, anomie, even madness. Just look around. Who in any kind of sane state would create a world where we can obliterate all of humanity? Or foul our drinking water? Or contaminate the air? Or reduce nutrients in food? Or educate at the highest levels to increase greed? Or allow millions to suffer in refugee camps? Collectively, we have created an awful set of conditions for ourselves and for our fellows.

Carl Jung may have identified the problem some time ago in *Civilization in Transition*, "As scientific understanding has grown, so our world has become dehumanized. Man feels himself isolated in the cosmos, because he is no longer involved in nature and has lost his emotional "unconscious identity" with natural phenomena… Thunder is no longer the voice of an angry god, nor is lightening the avenging missile. No river contains a spirit, no tree is the principle of life in man, no snake contains the embodiment of wisdom, no mountain cave is the home of a demon. No voices now speak to man from stones, plants or animals, nor does he speak to them believing they can hear. His contact with nature has gone and with it has gone the profound emotional energy that this symbolic connection supplied"

Real change is hard, as anyone who has tried to change her behavior knows from experience. Change gets exponentially more difficult at the level of competing interests in the total society. Sometimes it is just easier to deny reality than to change our worldview unless we get really sick or have to change fundamentally unhealthy habits like over-consuming alcohol, overeating, or smoking. And sometimes, old beliefs persist, regardless of the evidence to the contrary. "Despite certain events of the twentieth century, most people in the Western cultural tradition still believe in the Victorian idea of progress."[1] The belief in progress manifests as the notion that problems we face will simply go away through the application of a new technology or the belief that there will be some other fix. But what would the solution to the problem be if we found the cause of our current condition to be virtually everything: the economic and political system, agriculture, science, education, industry, medicine and just about every other facet of our civilization?

For some, hitting bottom is the only way to finally force the necessary change in behavior. If so, then the question becomes, " How far is bottom?" How many hurricanes, wildfires, floods, extinctions, and so on will it take to wake up? How many or what kind of dramatic event or events do we need to see the bottom? Naomi Klein describes the dilemma many of us face. "What makes carbon pollution such a stubborn problem: we can't see it, so we don't really believe it exists. Ours is culture of disavowal of simultaneously knowing and not knowing – the illusion of proximity coupled with the reality of distance is the trick perfected by the fossil-fuel global market. So we both know and don't know who makes our goods, who cleans up after us, where our waste disappears to - whether it's our sewage or electronics or our carbon emissions."[2] Because the worst risks of climate change are at least fifty years away, the actions of today won't be felt for a couple of decades. As Ronald Wright notes, "Even if abundant sources of clean energy were to come on stream tomorrow, we would still face problems of overpopulation, overconsumption, soil erosion and the most unequal distribution of wealth and health in history."[3] With our culturally adolescent outlook that measures value in the immediate future instead of that of a mature adult who looks at the results affecting several generations hence, the cost now is considered to be too much to invest in the future of our civilization. What is lost with this attitude is that we don't see how our system can change by taking action now. "The {current} system is in no one's interest. It is a suicide machine...The reform that is needed is not anti-capitalist, anti-American, or even deep environmentalist; it is simply the transition from short-term to long-term thinking. From recklessness and excess to moderation and the precautionary principle."[4] This simple understanding eludes too many of us – or we choose to ignore it.

The truth of the matter is that those in the minority who are comfortably well-off and politically powerful find it much easier to see that we are still on the grand march of progress. Very little disturbs their lifestyle. The consequences of resource extraction on the planet simply do not apply to them.

The privileged minority gets most of the benefits in the current reality and are shielded in a bubble from the suffering caused to those not so protected. As Rinaldo Brutoco notes, "Hunger, poverty, social and economic injustice, global warming, resource depletion, pollution, overpopulation, the loss of rain forests – all these factors are escalating and are now tending to converge in catastrophe… The global financial system that was wrapped around this inequitable distribution of goods and services is itself coming apart... What we have for a certainty is an economic system in great jeopardy of collapse because it is destroying the planet and leaving far too many people desperate, hungry, thirsty, and uneducated – and far too may children dead – and those tragic statistics are worsening every day. At every level, the economic system isn't working for the vast majority of the seven billion people on the planet."[5]

You might think we only need to extract more resources to address the inequalities in the world, but you would be mistaken. The very fact that we have so many fossil fuel resources still in the ground is cause for concern. That is, if we actually extract all the fossil fuels available, we could essentially create a rival to the scorching climate found on Venus.[6]

The oil and gas industry understands quite well that continuing in its current form provides the profits they stand to lose. If the system transitions to a green consciousness, they lose substantially. They have almost no incentive to change; the cost to the bottom line, the only measure in business that matters, is too high. And having oil company CEOs torn to pieces by howling mobs won't actually do much for humanity, the planet, or future generations since the issue is much larger. It is not an overstatement to note that, "Our economy is at war with many forms of life on earth, including human life."[7]

When we realize that we are destroying thousands of acres of non-regenerating forests, and that un-numbered species are going extinct each month because we indulge in so many excesses, "we can hardly be surprised by the amount of epidemic illness in our culture, from increasingly severe immune dysfunctions and cancers, to widespread psychological distress, depression, and ever more frequent suicides, to the accelerating number of household killings and mass murders committed for no apparent reason by otherwise coherent individuals."[8] We have to remember -- everything is connected.

The oil and gas industry is not the only culprit; again, all of us are complicit as well. As Gregg Branden notes, "It takes a lot of fuel to produce our food. It takes energy to drive the tractors to plow and prepare the land and plant the seeds. While the crops are growing, it takes fuel to create the electricity to pump water from the well to the irrigation systems to keep the plants alive. It takes fuel to run the tractors and huge combines at harvest time to gather the produce. It takes fuel to run the conveyors that move, sort, and prepare the produce for markets; and of course, it takes fuel to power the vehicles that get the product from where it's grown to our local market."[9] Our culpability is every bit as real as the demonized corporate transnationals, as Ronald Wright notes, "We tend to think of the looming energy crisis in terms of cars, factories, heating and air conditioning, but the first thing to keep in mind is that fossil fuels are feeding us. We all know that coal and oil drive the tractors, trains, trucks, ships and freezers that grow, store and move food from farm to city, nation to nation. But how many are aware that we have literally been eating oil and gas for more than a hundred years? Fossil carbon is a prime ingredient of the artificial fertilizers that have sidestepped the decline of natural fertility each time a crop is taken off a field. A two-century carbon binge has allowed mankind to fill its planet way beyond the natural carrying capacity of feckless, reckless, self-indulgent apes."

Before closing, let's look at a few more examples. One is from a report by a team of mathematicians, natural and social scientists from NASA's Goddard Space Flight Center whose central finding is that modern civilization is doomed. They warn us that, "the convergence of food, water and energy crises could create a 'perfect storm' within about fifteen years."

Even though most of us who are comfortably in the middle class don't see the problems in any personal way, we are reminded by Homer-Dixon that "The crumbling of the world order we depend on, if and when it happens, is most likely to begin at its margins."[10]

This jeremiad by Graham Hancock sums up the issue. "Our pollution and neglect of the majestic garden of the earth, our rape of its resources, our abuse of the oceans and the rainforests, our fear, hatred and suspicion of one another multiplied by a hundred bitter regional and sectarian conflicts, our consistent record of standing by and doing nothing while millions suffer, our ignorant, narrow-minded racism, our exclusivist religions, our forgetfulness that we are all brothers and sisters, our bellicose chauvinism, the dreadful cruelties that we indulge in, in the name of nation, or faith, or simple greed, our obsessive, competitive, ego-driven production and consumption of material goods and the growing conviction of many, fuelled by the triumphs of materialist science, that matter is all there is – that there is no such thing as spirit, that we are just accidents of chemistry and biology – all these things, and many more in mythological terms at least, do not look good for us."[11]

Given all of the problems and issues afflicting contemporary society, one has to ask, "Is this the end, that is, the collapse of civilization as we know it?" Of course the answer varies according to who answers the question. For many who are going about their lives as if nothing is seriously wrong – their lives are just fine, thank you. More likely they think the idea of collapse is just the ridiculous fancy of an elite few. For those who envision a world without a reliance on fossil fuels and other extracted resources, the temptation to see a collapse is almost a foregone conclusion.

Whether one believes in the adequacy of the conditions of civilization as it is or believes in the need for a major change if we are to survive, the verdict is still out; no one knows the future. Trends have been upset in the past; new and unforeseen developments are always in play. That said, there is ample evidence that our way of being is in serious crisis and is cause for alarm, regardless of belief. Even if there is no immediate collapse, we have to address the mounting problems of our current unsustainable basis for civilized society.

The truth is that every great civilization has collapsed and there is no reason to assume ours won't eventually. So, it is in our best interests to study this matter and develop whatever strategies we need to avoid what has been the historical fate of all great civilizations. In days of old in the coal mines, the condition of the canary's health in the mine was the signal for danger to the miners in the tunnels. In a similar way, we have an abundance of environmental canaries whose health is very much in question and we best heed their messages. We know that once the fundamental structures underpinning the culture's systems fray, the collapse is virtually unstoppable. Think back to the fall of Europe's Communist block, for example. The Soviet Union seemed as permanent in 1985 as ours does today. The transformation that occurred in the Soviet Union seemed to happen overnight historically. What appears to be substantial can be as ephemeral as the wind.

Safa Motesharrei, an applied mathematician who was with the National Socio-Environmental Synthesis Center At NASA's Goddard Space flight Center, performed a detailed study of the following five risk factors as they impact society: population, climate, water, agriculture and energy. He reported that all societal collapses over the past five thousand years fell into two categories: the ecological system that couldn't support the culture, and the elites of the time who accumulated resources for themselves and restricted resources accessable to the masses. (Sound familiar?)

Part of the reason for concern is not simply a matter of the supply and distribution of resources. Once the fundamental and fragile beliefs of a people evaporate, once there is no longer a "belief in the rightness of its values; belief in the strength of its system of law and order; belief in its currency; above all, perhaps, belief in its future" then a corrosive cancer eats away the culture. [12] Once any significant portion of the system stops working, the concept of "irreducible complexity" – all parts must work to keep the system alive -- takes over and the entire system shuts down.

"Civilizations take time to fall; the resource base of industrial society is shrinking but it's far from exhausted; the impact of global warming and other ecological disruptions build slowly over time; and ruling elites and ordinary citizens alike have every reason to hold things together as long as possible."[13] and yet, Motesharrei's report concludes that "closely reflecting the reality of the world today ... we find that collapse is difficult to avoid." About the study, NASA commented, "As is the case with all independent research, the views and conclusions in the paper are those of the authors alone. NASA does not endorse the paper or its conclusions."

The case for continued use of fossil fuels is not without support. Let's not forget that "Fossil fuels have shaped every facet or our lives, right down to our thoughts, hopes and dreams. These hopes and dreams are molded with petroleum oil, just as plastic is."[14] We can continue on our current resource use path regardless of consequences for some time ahead. As David Keith writes, "Come when it may, the end of easy oil will not signal a shortage of fossil fuels or of energy. We have sufficient resources of coal, gas and unconventional oil to power our fossil–driven civilization at twice our current burn rate for more than two centuries."[15] Those looking for alternate energy sources often suggest we can rely on windmills to generate power. This is a questionable solution. "At a good wind site, the energy payback day could be in three years or less; in a poor location, energy payback may be never. That is, a windmill could spin until it falls apart and never generate as much energy as was invested in building it."[16] The truth is that given our appetite for energy use, there is really no good alternative for oil.

The choice appears to be that we can continue on the path we're on for quite a while and those in the future will suffer the eventual consequences or we can envision a completely new system, one not based solely on fossil fuels. Any seriously major change in our lifestyle is likely to be catastrophic since we are so embedded in the myth of cheap oil forever. Perhaps the biggest threat when thinking about a significant change is the loss of jobs, jobs that are totally dependent on the way society is organized now. We certainly can't just stop mills from running, oil from being pumped, fish from being farmed, and lumber from being cut, as well as a host of other ways people work to support their families without disastrous consequences. What seems more practical is to begin to wean ourselves away from our current dependence on fossil fuels and other limited resources. A series of thoughtful, staged retreats over time would allow us to adjust to a new reality. To do otherwise is to be reminded of an old Cree prophecy: When the last tree is cut down, the last fish eaten, and the last stream poisoned, you will realize that you cannot eat money.

The likely choice – do we or don't we make the necessary choices now? -- may well be the one Ronald Wright noted when he wrote, "The truth is that human beings drove themselves out of Eden, and they have done it again and again by fouling their own nests… Many of the great ruins that grace the deserts and jungles of the earth are monuments to progress traps, the headstones of civilizations which fell victim to their own success." For some, there is little room for optimism. For others, however, "Hope springs eternal from the human breast." Yes, there is room for hope and not just pie-in-the-sky hope, but that's a perspective we will consider in another chapter.

Fossil Fuels endnotes

1. Wright, Wright, Ronald, <u>A Short History of Progress</u> (2004), House of Anansi Press Inc., Toronto, Ontario, Canada, p. 3.

2.Klein, Naomi, <u>This Changes Everything: Capitalism vs. The Climate</u> (2014), Alfred A. Knopf, Canada, p. 168.

3. From the Forward, Ronald Wright, in Homer-Dixon, Thomas and Garrison, Nick, <u>Carbon Shift: How the Twin Crises of Oil Depletion and Climate Change Will Define the Future</u> (2009), Random House of Canada p. ix.

4. Wright, Wright, Ronald, <u>A Short History of Progress</u> (2004), House of Anansi Press Inc., Toronto, Ontario, Canada, p. 131.

5. "Ascent of the Phoenix: Global Reconstruction", Rinaldo Brutoco, in Hubbard, Barbara, Marx, <u>Birth 2012 And Beyond: Humanity's Great Shift to the Age of Conscious Evolution</u> (2012), Shift Books, p. 179.

6. "Dangerous Abundance", Keith, David, Homer-Dixon, Thomas and Garrison, Nick, <u>Carbon Shift: How the Twin Crises of Oil Depletion and Climate Change Will Define the Future</u> (2009), Random House of Canada, p. 28.

7. Klein, 2014, p. 21.

8. Abram, Abram, David, <u>The Spell of the Sensuous: Perception and Language in a More-Than-Human World</u> (1997), Vintage Books, NY, p. 22.

9. Braden, Gregg, <u>The Turning Point: Creating Resilience in a Time of Extremes</u> (2014), Hay House, NY, NY, p. 72.

10. Homer-Dixon, Homer-Dixon, Thomas, <u>The Upside of Down: Catastrophe, Creativity, and the Renewal of Civilization</u> (2007), Homer-Dixon, Thomas, Vintage Canada, Toronto, Canada, p. 174.

11. Hancock, Hancock, Graham, <u>Magicians Of The Gods</u> (2015), Coronet Pub, UK pp. 426-427.

12. Dark Mountain Project, http://dark-mountain.net/about/manifesto/

13. Greer, John Michael, Getting Beyond the Narratives: An Open Letter to the Activist Community, (2005), http://www.ecosophia.net/getting-beyond-narratives/

14."The Perfect Moment", Marsden, William, in <u>Carbon Shift</u>, 2009, p. 154-155.

15. "Dangerous Abundance", Keith, David, in <u>Carbon Shift</u>, 2009, p. 30.

16. Keith, David, 2009, p. 71.

17.Wright, 2004, pp. 8-9.

4

Language

The written word appeared about 6000 yeas ago and significantly altered our perception of time. We are used to the written word and probably many of us don't notice how it continuously shapes our perceptions. But the written word was not always the case. For non-literate peoples, time was cyclical, with ever returning seasons. With the written word, time became linear and historical, divorced from the harmony of recurring natural rhythms. The perception of time went from a mythic connection with the natural world to one in which time was sequential and historical. As Paul Shepard noted, "The phonetic alphabet, pictorial space, and Euclidean geometry are not just ideas and formulas; they are representations supporting a linear view of the world that in turn shapes our experience on the nonlinear natural world and its creatures."

Written language is powerful. Without written language there could be no civilization as we know it. As Charles Eisenstein observed, "Language is prior to any technology requiring the accumulation of knowledge and the coordination of human activity. Anything human civilization has ever created, from the pyramids to the space station, rests ultimately upon a foundation of symbols." We have come to understand and use words to have objective meanings; we see words as independent of readers and writers, speakers and listeners; they have become objects themselves. Perhaps nothing was more reinforcing of the value of words as objects than the invention of the printing press, which increased the use of written language by several orders of magnitude.

Yet, for all the differences in perception between old oral cultures and that of the contemporary world, the written world speaks to us in much the same way that Nature once spoke to our forebears. As David Abram wrote, "As nonhuman animals, plants and even 'inanimate' rivers once spoke to our tribal ancestors, so the 'inert' letters on the page now speak to us! It is a form of animism that we take for granted, but it is animism nonetheless – as mysterious as a talking stone… It is only when a culture shifts its participation to these printed letters that the stones fall silent. Only as our senses transfer their animating magic to the written word do the trees become mute, the other animals dumb."

The Greeks and Hebrews did much to move our spiritual sensibilities from the rhythms of Nature to the heavens. Plato's eternal non-physical forms were located in some ethereal realm beyond physical reality; the Hebrews located the highest spirit in the sky, far away from the Earth's recurring cycles. This shift, again, from David Abram, "contributed profoundly to civilization's distrust of bodily and sensorial experience, and to our consequent estrangement from the earthly world around us." No longer was human speech connected to a vast reality; humans spoke only to each other; no longer did the Earth speak. The very air was stripped of its psychic depth, its invisible influences. We forgot, as John Michael Greer reminds us that, "every name is an abstraction imposed on a complex reality, and to treat the name as though it's an independent reality lurching around all by itself causing problems — that's reification, and it's fatal." Our world is infinitely more complex than mere words would have us believe. Perhaps nowhere else than in science is this known to be the case. Scientists, who are consistently discovering more subtle aspects of the workings of the cosmos, are forever revising the language they use when discussing what they find in Nature. It may be, as Eric Weiner whimsically noted, "We cherish the hidden more than the exposed. That is why God invented wrapping paper and lingerie." In spite of our dependence upon the written word to denote reality, the world still contains mysteries.

We have continued to divorce our lives from our connection with Nature at our own peril. Just how that peril is manifesting currently is the topic of the next chapter.

5

Transformation

In the pre-Enlightenment version (which was before the 1700s), the early Christian mythological view held that there is God at the apex of the pyramid of human understanding of divinity. Below Him, Satan and a couple of angels occupied the ethers; all other spirits were dismissed as pagan aberrations, and at bottom in the world of humans was the word of God as inscribed in the Bible. The Bible was meant to explain everything and guide humans to eternal life through this vale of tears on Earth. Humans existed to adore and serve God. This view shaped much of the experience of those living before the Enlightenment. Shortly after the Enlightenment, when God was dethroned and replaced by man as the crown of creation, Satan, the angels and spirits were dispensed with, and the new science replaced revealed scripture as human's guide to the good life. Now the human being sitting at the pinnacle determined the fate of all that was below. And the guide to life itself, written by humans, was to be as essential to the modern sensibility as was the fundamentalist literal scripture of yesteryear. The journey of man to be one with God turned into man's journey of Progress through science.

The new science –although it brought amazing benefits to the human community -- became as inflexible and intolerant of any other perspective in the same way as the previous scripture. In this way, both guides, if you will, shared a fundamentally doctrinaire perspective, the religious one rooted in the world of spirit; science, rooted in the other, the substantial world of matter. The content of the guide changed, but the dynamic did not. Structurally, both were mirrors of each and shared an ethos of dogmatism. Neither invited a transformation of vision and purpose. Neither included an awesome respect or connection with Nature, the Earth, and other animals. Science just took over the attitude of religion, which was as David Abrams notes, "The Church had long assumed that only human beings have intelligent souls, and that the other animals, to say nothing of trees and rivers, were 'created' for no other reason than to serve humankind."[1] The new science had the very same perspective.

From the Enlightenment onward, everything only existed to serve humankind, which had replaced the Godhead. And now to bring us up to current times, it seems appropriate to quote Laurel and Hardy once again, "What a fine mess you've gotten us into." Welcome to the march of scientific progress we call modernity, a topic whose history is worth exploring in a short digression.

Before the Enlightenment there was no individual identity as we think of that idea; who you were had to do with loyalties to which authority figure dominated: the local chief, or lord. We take personal identity as given, that is, we have some notion that who we are is somehow special, unique. Back then, a person's identity was not a choice; if a person did have a particular identity, it was always connected to one's occupation, social class, or other some designation that was not chosen or could be changed. That way of being was reinforced through the hierarchal structure of the town, village, or fiefdom where the person lived. "The duty of persons in authority was to maintain the official worldview; that of everybody else, to conform to it."[2] The individual was only aware of inherited tradition. The most any person would ever expect is more of the same as it had always been. There was not a sense of linear progress and change, only an awareness of the ever-present ongoing cycle of life. There were no immigrants, no peoples from different cultures, no significant "others" who had a different worldview to challenge the values and traditions of the community. Except for a literate few of the elite, illiteracy was the norm. For most of the folks of this period, there were no books, no ideas to challenge local sources, and no way to see the world outside of the narrow views of the community.

Christian myths dominated the imagination. The church was all-powerful in its power to explain whatever needed explanation and provided the dominant myths around which village or tribal life was conducted. Here is what Arthur Schlesinger, Jr. had to say about religion in that time, "The great religious ages were notable for their indifference to human rights in the contemporary sense. They were notorious not only for acquiescence in poverty, inequality, exploitation and oppression but for enthusiastic justifications of slavery, persecution, abandonment of small children, torture, genocide. . . Religion enshrined and vindicated hierarchy, authority and inequality and had no compunction about murdering heretics and blasphemers."[3] Without equivocation, one could say there was certainly a brutish aspect of the pre-modern, pre-Enlightenment period.

What was considered objective reality was identical to what the social belief system said it was. In short, while scholars and historians may point to a variety of political and military forces that were subtlety influencing and changing the period over time, for our purposes the pre-modern period as we see it now evolved so slowly we may say that in effect, it was essentially static.

Reading the history of the modern period, from the Enlightenment to the present, one could easily think that somehow the scholars and thinkers in the 18th century woke up and re-discovered science and the ancient Greek and Roman texts all in one fell swoop and created what we now call the Great Enlightenment, but of course, that is not exactly what happened. What happened exactly would take more detail than I wish to go into, so let it suffice to say that the Enlightenment happened and there were lots of reasons for it, not the least of which was the earlier invention of the Gutenberg Press in the 15th century, which brought literacy to the masses.

From the 18th century to the present, we in the West have been in an increasingly and thoroughly modern world, one verging, or if not already in, the postmodern period. But before getting too far ahead, let's look at the early modern revolution born of the Enlightenment.

The early modern period birthed rational thought and empirical observation, what we now call the scientific method. Science began its ascendance as the primary mode of discovering real knowledge and is today regarded as the gold standard of knowledge. The promise of the scientific method suggested to many that there was no doubt that absolute truth was discoverable, and that progress toward a more perfect society was achievable and inevitable because of rational inquiry (no sloppy thinking), careful methodical discipline, and reliance on empirical observation (hard facts). The problems afflicting humanity would be solved by the application of science and technology. The now de-mystified material world became the province of science. And increasingly, especially in our time, science replaced religion as the source of absolute truth for many in the educated classes.

Science soon became the dominant force in the Enlightenment. Virtually everyone believed in progress. European modernists had a dependable path to truth, and the truth included grand myths of superior European cultural and ethnic origins, which were accepted as received. Impressive theories explaining how Europeans (and later, white Americans) became the most civilized, cultured, and powerful peoples were solidified.

Human rights came with modernism. "Human rights is not a religious idea. It is a secular idea, the product of the last four centuries of Western history. The basic human rights documents – the American Declaration of Independence and the French Declaration of the Rights of Man – were written by political, not by religious leaders. And the revival of absolutism in recent times, whether in religious or secular form, has brought with it the revival of torture, of slaughter and other monstrous violation of human rights."[4] Over time, other ideas from the Enlightenment -- like individual autonomy, liberty, and independence became standard in all modern societies. Marxism and competitive corporate culture, both outgrowths of democratic capitalism, developed in the Industrial Revolution. Both were a modernist creation. And today, only a country that is essentially modernist in outlook can sustain a functional democracy.[5]

The rise of modernism as the dominant intellectual, social, and artistic sensibility also had a less attractive aspect. A world devoid of any sort of non-material "presence" in nature, any sense of ultimate human purpose, and any valuing system beyond mechanical expediency created the very conditions that have been causing a re-evaluation of its schema. The failure of predictable social progress (especially WWI & WWII), the disenchantment with the grand narratives of racial superiority, the breakthroughs in the study of language, and the overwhelming success of modernism itself created a re-evaluation of thinking that is called post-modernity.

Another significant development that moved science from modernism to post modernism is the shift regarding reality from a Newtonian to a Quantum perspective. It is no longer a meaningful concept to think that the universe is a giant machine, which is a modernist idea; rather, one of the emerging views is that the universe is characterized as having a grand intelligence. The current scientific paradigm is that our intent as an observer affects what we observe: there is no specific "way that reality is". Rather the "way reality is" is always a probability. Lots of possibilities and probabilities exist; reality is changeable, it is not absolute. The human being was brought forth as a significant player in the business of determining what reality can be. And with that, somehow everything changed. We woke up and found we lived in a disenchanted world, a world simmering with the failed promise of predictable progress.

In our time the tremendous gaps in the belief in the inevitably of progress became too large to ignore. And yet, from the early twentieth century to today, the idealism of inevitable progress continues to fall apart even as some have forgotten that progress, human centrality, separation from nature and spirit is a dysfunctional myth inherited from a past that no longer exists; many of us forgot that it was only a story we told ourselves far too often. "The best minds of our time are telling us that we are already in crisis, and actually facing multiple critical situations all happening a the same time -- now."[6] All one has to do is take a look (as we have been doing relentlessly in this text). Good-bye rain forests, fertile soil, clean rivers, fish in the oceans, ice sheets, abundant resources; hello desertification, extreme weather – hurricanes, droughts, wild fires, rising sea levels, insect infestations -- carbon emissions, permanent war, world hunger, massive population shifts and so on. The list, tiresomely long, is a reminder that climate change, for example "is already here, increasingly brutal disasters are headed our way, no matter what we do."[7]

What is clear is that the old systems and ideas and consciousness about how to live are not serving us anymore. We cannot go back to the way things used to be. They were never sustainable. This realization is difficult for the ordinary person to get. As Gregg Braden observed, "Now is different. The world that we grew up with is gone, and it's not coming back. It disappeared before our eyes. While we were shopping for the weekly groceries, putting meals on the table for our families, and caring for our aging parent, the familiar world we've known and trusted disappeared. The trouble is that no one told us this was happening. No one told us that our lives were being changed forever."[8] We are in crisis because we have lost our way in the world. One consequence is to deny any of this is happening or has happened, or to see it as a temporary bump in the road of progress, a technical glitch. Another is to recognize where we are. As the writers of Dark Mountain noted, "Today's generation are demonstrably less content, and consequently less optimistic, than those that went before. They work longer hours, with less security, and less chance of leaving behind the social background into which they were born. They fear crime, social breakdown, overdevelopment, and environmental collapse. They do not believe that the future will be better than the past. Individually, they are less constrained by class and convention than their parents or grandparents, but more constrained by law, surveillance, state proscription and personal debt."[9]

The evidence is clear. However, how do we address what needs to happen? Barbara Marx Hubbard tells us that, "We have reached what systems theorists call a 'chaos point.' When a system in chaos is far from equilibrium, it tries to right itself by going backward to the old; this is why we see reactive movements everywhere in society right now. But an evolving system cannot return to the past. It must seek out new structures and systems, and quickly ascend to a new configuration – or else face rapid decline."[10] As you might expect, there is no shortage of suggestions; they involve:

moving from consumer materialism to valuing quality of life; moving from "I-It" relationship to others to an "I-Thou" consciousness; moving away from exploitation of the Earth to sustainability; moving away from environmental destruction; moving away from bigger, better, and more to sharing; moving to embrace our connection with Nature and Spirit; moving to collaboration and away from competition; moving from separation to connection; moving toward equality for all and away from dominance; moving toward the identity of "all that is" as aspects of the divine. These are only some of the more obvious directions of the choices before us.

But let's move away from the particular suggestions and take another perspective, one that might be more amenable to personal practical action. Before we do that, however, let's keep a couple of ideas from Barbara Marx Hubbard in mind. "Crisis almost always precedes transformation… The process of transformation is not linear." Almost always for change to take place, some precipitating event or significant event has to spur movement from where one is to a movement away from where one is. In theory we could make a quantum leap, but more cautiously, I'd add quickly that all huge ideas move slowly and often awkwardly if they move at all. In the case of major cultural change, the systems are so interconnected and tightly linked together that no transformation is apt to happen overnight even though the change may seem inevitable to those working for the transformation to happen. After all, what is being envisioned is a reconceiving of who we are – a much deeper effort is in play -- as we work to reverse the crisis of our times. Our deeper need is to get in touch with that which has been, if not lost, at least repressed for a long time. Paul Shepard reminds us, "We have become accustomed to identifying a wide range of physical and social disorders – everything from war to ethnic intolerance, stress and trauma disorders, epidemic disease, and the vague dissatisfactions that lead to addictions and suicide – as weaknesses in the social political, or technological order, rather than as evidence of a deep, ecological dissociation from our genetic core." Our genetic core was formed over thousands of years, as we know. There may be a number of ways to get to that core. I'm suggesting that we have to re-connect with Nature and learn how to read it. Joseph Needleman writes, "The earth is a sacred book. An ancient idea – found almost everywhere in the ancient worlds, from Pharaonic Egypt to the alchemists and esoteric visionaries of Judaism, Christianity and Islam; to the Taoism of China and the hidden doctrines and practices in the mountains of Tibet and in the surpassingly great cultures of India, to the powerful spiritual teaching of tribal cultures throughout the Americas, Africa, Asia: Nature in all its diversity as the signature of God and, indeed, the 'language' of God. A language that has both an inner and outer meaning, like scripture itself."[12]

Now all of that is fine and good, you might say, but how, as a practical matter am I to do all of that? For the answer to that question, I need to digress for a moment to an example supplied by Tom Chi, in a TED talk in October, 2015, entitled, "Everything is Connected," who reminds us that the breath we take for granted because it is so abundant was made possible by the work of billions of miniscule single celled cyanobacteria who, using chemosynthesis over millions of years to convert carbon dioxide to oxygen (in the form of ozone), eventually created a world we could live in. Before oxygen was created there was no multicellular life, a necessary phenomenon which had to evolve before we could evolve. These bacteria performed yeoman service. Quite literally, we owe our lives to these simple bacteria doing a very simple action over time. Their work is a reminder that the meaning of our lives or the purpose of our lives may not be in the scope of our immediate lives or understanding anymore than the fruit of all those cyanobacteria in producing the conditions for life as we know it was to them. What we do today may seriously affect the future in ways we cannot see. We live in a palette of colors created by our bacteria predecessors. We, in turn, create a palette of colors for the future. We change the future by our choices. All of which is to say, our choices, seeming small and insignificant, matter to those who follow us.

Our frame of mind may need to expand beyond that of adolescent consciousness which is normally directed at quick results, or that of the corporate executive who is only looking at the balance sheet for the next nearest quarter, to that of the mature adult, who looks generations forward. "It has been said that our generation is the first in history that can decide whether it's the last in history. We need to add that our generation is also the first in history that can decide whether it will be the first generation of a new phase in history."[13] We are not likely to change history by fighting existing reality; we have to build a new model to send the old model into the dustbin of history. As Charles Eisenstein reminds us, "Every act of generosity is an invitation into generosity. Every act of courage is an invitation into courage. Every act of selflessness is an invitation into selflessness. Every act of healing is an invitation into healing… Whether invisible or not, acts of great faith, acts that come from a stance deep in the territory of reunion, send powerful ripples out through the fabric of causality. One way or another, perhaps via pathways we are unaware of, they surface in the visible world."[16]

As the cliché from Gandhi tells us, "Be the change you want to see." Each of us has to ask ourselves "What does the world I want to live in look like?" and then go about our daily lives enacting the behaviors and attitudes that may bring it into being even if that doesn't happen in our personal lifetime. Remembering that "Utopia will not be achieved by better science, more precise technology, finer control over inner or outer reality. It will not happen by trying harder to be good and not by better controlling nature or human nature... It is only by transcending that program and its accompanying conception of self that we can expect to create anything other than a further intensification of what we have today."[17]

Transformation endnotes

1. Abram, David, <u>The Spell of the Sensuous: Perception and Language in a More-Than-Human World</u> (1997), Vintage Books, NY, p. 8.

2. Anderson, Walter Truett, <u>Reality Isn't What It Used To Be: Theatrical Politics, Ready-to-Wear Religion, Global Myths, Primitive Chic, and Other Wonders of the Postmodern world</u>. (1990), HaperSanFransico, CA, p. 70.

3. Schlesinger, Jr, The Opening of the American Mind," Arthur Schlesinger, Jr. in <u>The Truth About The Truth: De-Confusing and Re-Constructing The Postmodern World</u>, 1995.p. 226.

4. Schlesinger, 1995, p. 226.

5. McIntosh, Steve, <u>Integral Consciousness And The Future Of Evolution: How The Integral Worldview Is Transforming Politics, Culture, And Spirituality</u> (2007), Paragon House, St. Paul, MN, p. 112.

6. (Braden, Gregg, <u>Deep Truth: Igniting the Memory of Our origin, History, Destiny, and Fate</u> (2011), Hay House, NY, NY, p. 78.

7. Klein, Naomi, <u>This Changes Everything: Capitalism vs. The Climate</u> (2014), Alfred A. Knopf, Canada, p. 28.

8. Braden, Gregg, <u>The Turning Point: Creating Resilience in a Time of Extremes</u> (2014), Hay House, NY, NY, p. 3.

9. Dark Mountain Project, <u>http://dark - mountain.net/about/manifesto/</u>

10. Hubbard, Barbara, Marx, <u>Birth 2012 And Beyond: Humanity's Great Shift to the Age of Conscious Evolution</u> (2012), Shift Books, p. 5.

11. Homer-Dixon, Thomas, <u>The Upside of Down: Catastrophe, Creativity, and the Renewal of Civilization</u> (2007), Homer-Dixon, Thomas, Vintage Canada, Toronto, Canada, p. 125.

12. Needleman, Jacob, <u>An Unknown World: Notes on The Meaning of The Earth</u> (2012), Jeremy P. Tarcher/Penguiun, NY, pp. 33-34.

13. Laszlo, Ervin, Global Bifurcation: The 2012 Decision Window, Ervin Laszlo, in Hubbard, 2012, p. 146.

14. Eisenstein, Charles, <u>The More Beautiful World Our Hearts Know is Possible</u> (2013), North Atlantic Books, Berkeley, CA, pp. 60 & 204.

15. Eisenstein, Charles, <u>The Ascent of Humanity: Civilization and the Human Sense of Self</u> (2007), Evolver Editions, North Atlantic Books, Berkeley, CA, p. 394.

6

Earth

We have all seen a movie or TV program with a patient in hospital garb either in the intensive care unit or in the operating room. Her blood sample has been taken, various tissues have been biopsied, several gauges are monitoring her various biological systems, and she has an oxygen hose applied to her nose. All sorts of uniformed personnel are busy attending to her. We know just by looking at her that all is not well. We may wonder, "Will she survive? Or will we have a dead body?"

Given that scientists all over the world are hovering over their instruments monitoring air quality, taking water samples, examining soil, measuring glaciation, wind currents, tectonic plate movement, volcanic eruptions, deep fissures in the oceans, wildlife habitats, species extinction, and tropical forest depletion, as well as taking other measurements more-or-less continuously, is there any doubt that we are looking at a critically ill planet? We may ask the same question of the Earth as we have of the hospital patient, "Will she survive? Or will we have a dead body?"

We know the Earth will continue its existence whether there is life on the planet or not. Of course, it will not have the same self-regulating set of systems that support human and other forms of life, but the planet, absent life as we know it now, will continue to orbit the sun as it has for millennia. Before addressing that question -- "Will the patient survive, and if so, what will its quality of life be?"-- it behooves us to know more about this patient, Earth, so we have a much better idea of just what is at stake regarding her health. Let's get all the information we can so we may treat the illness with some practical approaches that may lead to healing.

Children and adolescents may receive some education about our planet in Earth Science or even in Social Studies, but in the main, most adults have long since forgotten most of what was taught to them in those early years. These days, what we know of the Earth mostly comes from the media, with TV being the most accessed for information. We hear of a variety of natural disasters, the dangers of climate change (or its deniers), and the like, but what do people really understand about our relationship to the planet, quite literally our birth mother? This will take a bit of digging, but with some attention, we may come to appreciate just how precious our Earth is and what a privilege it is to be able to live here. Perhaps with an increased appreciation of all that the Earth provides so we may enjoy living here, we will be more willing to act like the loving competent caretakers we can be.

Beginnings

As with all living things, the Earth over time has changed. Once upon a time, the Earth had a twin, Theia, which was about half as wide as the Earth. The Earth and Thea collided. The planet Earth merged with planet Theia in space. What was left of the union became what we now know as the Earth, and the debris became what is now our moon.[1] All that happened about 4.5 billion years ago. Since then the continents have drifted apart and come together as supercontinents perhaps six times as the twenty or so tectonic plates shifted positions adjusting to the heat beneath in the core of the Earth. They are still shifting. Mountains rose and fell. "The ice cover waxed and waned; global temperatures rose and fell; species emerged, evolved and became extinct."[2] At first, no life existed. Then about 3.5 billion years ago, single celled bacteria arrived – just how they did is addressed later in this chapter --making the climate comfortable for the establishment of human and other forms of life.

In the relatively recent past, given the age of the Earth, an ice-sheet 40,000 years in the making melted away within a period of 2,000 years, bringing us up to about 12,000 years ago. And then another drastic change happened; "Some 11,500 years ago, the warming world must have plunged back into a mini ice age… The cold snap, now called the Younger Dryas (after a tundra plant that flourished across Europe at the time), lasted more than 1,000 years."[3] What happened exactly is still a matter of some dispute among scientists. The extreme returning of the cold climate could have been caused by a massive comet hitting the Earth in Siberia or a number of volcanoes much like the famous Krakotoa erupting elsewhere. While we don't usually think of comets hitting the Earth very often these days, in times past they may have hit the Earth every 100 years or so. The records indicate that, "there are 171 authenticated impact craters on Earth, the vast majority of these being on land."[4]

The impact on all living things when the comet hit the earth was extreme. Something like "thirty-five genera of mammals (with each genus consisting of several species) became extinct in North America between 12,900 and 11,600 years ago, i.e. precisely during the mysterious Younger Dryas cold event."[5] Somehow, shortly after this cataclysmic shock, the first signs of civilization -- Gobekli Tepe --arose in Turkey. Not long after, other sites around the world came into existence.[6] But I'm getting ahead of myself. Let's go back a bit.

The Earth has been positioned ideally to receive just the right amount of light and heat from an ideal sun for a very, very long time. And the moon added a stabilizing influence and tidal pull. As Stewart & Lynch, two science writers, for *National Geographic* noted, "It is incredible to think what a complicated and unlikely chain of events was needed to create a planet suitable for life. Earth had to be the right size and the right distance from the right kind of sun. It needed the right collision to create a moon for stability, the right protective planet in the wings, and just the right amount of water delivered from space. Add to that the right range of building materials, the correct amount of heat to make plate tectonics work, and the right chemistry to make our atmosphere and oceans conducive to life. All told, it is quite a feat to build a planet that is home to life – well, life that is more than simply bacterial slime. A planet like Earth might be very rare indeed."

And what a planet! One with diverse vegetation, widely variant climatic environments, a plethora of animals, moving air and sea currents, large and small bodies of salt and fresh water and so on. This amazing phenomenon, this planet full of life and dynamic energy, inspired Jacob Needleman, to write, "Earth science shows us the thick interrelationship between the planet and organic life, showing us that everything on Earth and the Earth itself is alive, showing us that the origin of life is life itself, the origin of the universe is the universe itself, and time and space are their own unfathomable origin."[7]

Exploring The Origins of Life

Let's get back to what may be the earliest forms of life and how they may have come to be. Current thinking has it that a kind of bacteria called extremophiles that live within the scalding volcanic springs under the ocean are related to the first organic life forms on the planet and are the distant ancestors of all the life that followed. Extremophiles have been on the planet for approximately three billion years. Initially, they probably survived by a process called chemosynthesis, which is the ability to extract nutrients from inorganic matter (remember: there was no organic matter according to this theory) and later developed the capacity to photosynthesize or get food from sunlight…We have no idea whether the microbes that flourish here are exactly like those that kick started life 4 billion years ago…These bacteria are in steamy volcanic wonderlands and frigid wastes of Antarctica, in deep mines and ocean mud hundred of yards beneath the sea floor.[8] We are indebted to the stromatolites and cyanobacteria, the extremophiles, for the creation of oxygen and protection from the sun's sterilizing rays. If not for their efforts over millions of years, we could not live on Earth.

Now the question is, how did these bacteria come to be? God? Chance? Or aliens? We know these bacteria can live in terribly hostile environments. We have pretty good evidence that they were here about 3.4 to 3.8 billion years ago, a mere 100 million or one half billion years from the 3.9 billion when the Earth's crust was fully formed. But according to Francis Compton Crick, codiscover of the structure of the DNA molecule and Nobel Prize recipient, and a man with strong mathematical skills, who noted that there was not nearly enough time to evolve DNA/RNA. "What bothered the statistician in Crick was the absolute improbability of even a single fully assembled protein made up of a long chain of amino acids emerging as a result of chance, -- no matter how nutritious the prebiotic soup or how many billions of years the ingredients were allowed to stew. Based on an average protein about 200 amino acids in length (others are much bigger), Crick calculated the odds of this happening as just one chance in a 1 followed by 260 zeros."[9] This was most troublesome to the arch-rationalist, seriously skilled mathematician and committed atheist. The appearance of life looked very like a miracle – there were so many conditions needed to get to the structure of the bacteria -- and he would have none of that. He decided bacteria were seeded on Earth by an extraterrestrial source and thrived in the climate into which they were put. Now it is true that organic materials have come to the Earth from comets, so his theory, called "panspermia" is not without some basis. There is some support for the possibility, at least in theory. Stewart and Lynch note that, "Interstellar space is replete with organic molecules, and that meteorites delivered these vital building blocks to the embryonic Earth. Whether or not life itself hitched a ride is still open to question, but if it did, there is every possibility that we are the offspring of Martians." And further, "Rich in the building blocks of life, the comets or asteroids that pummeled down are thought to have brought annual deliveries of 40 tons of amino acids and other organic molecules to the early Earth. What's more, as they smashed into Earth they released vast amounts of heat, perhaps kindling the first heat-loving organisms, thermophiles, which many biologist believe were the seedling for the tree of life."[10] However, regarding the beginning of life, we just don't know. Perhaps here is a place to consider the attitude of Einstein, who wrote, "The most beautiful thing we can experience is the mysterious… He to whom this emotion is a stranger, who can no longer pause to wonder and stand rapt in awe, is as good as dead: his eyes are closed. To know that what is impenetrable to us really exists, manifesting itself as the highest wisdom and the most radiant beauty which our dull faculties can comprehend only in their most primitive forms – this knowledge, this feeling is at the center of true religiousness. In this sense, and in this sense only, I belong to the ranks of devoutly religious men."

Earth Alive

Although many indigenous peoples and hunter-gatherers from the past viewed the Earth as alive, it was not until 2001 or thereabouts that scientists saw the Earth as a self-regulating entity. They did not see the Earth as a living being per se. James Lovelock coined the title "Gaia" as a metaphor for the self-regulating functions of the Earth. In spite of his hard materialist stance, he gets criticism for the concept of Gaia. When, in an interview, he was accused of going beyond the metaphor of Earth as Gaia, someone said to him, "You are doing it again –anthropomorphizing the Earth, talking of it as alive." But I say to them," if it is not alive then how can it die?" And die she will when the sun's heat becomes more than can be withstood."[12] Recognizing that there are several phenomena such as life itself, consciousness, and unexplainable events in quantum physics, many think Gaia is an accurate portrayal of a self-regulating Earth. They understand that many natural phenomena are not now understood and can't be easily explained using standard reductionist theory. What is important for all of us, Lovelock importunes is this: "Unless we see the Earth as a planet that behaves as if it were alive, at least to the extent of regulating its climate and chemistry, we will lack the will to change our way of life and to understand that we have made it our greatest enemy."[13]

The idea that the Earth is alive is longstanding even in the western philosophic tradition. Guy Murchie in *The Seven Mysteries of Life: An Exploration in Science and Philosophy* notes, "Greek philosophers of the sixth century B. C., who seem to have thought as deeply and with as little prejudice as any philosophers in history taught that life is a natural property of matter, an inevitable manifestation of the truth that the world has always been alive." But let's not forget that only about 400 years ago, Giordano Bruno was burned at the stake for maintaining that the Earth was alive. We have moved along philosophically.

Murchie makes the case that as germs or the many bacteria in the human body very likely do not know or have awareness that they live in such a body, how then can our comparable status in the total aliveness of the planet be significantly different? He goes on to raise the question, "If a mammal can maintain its life by keeping its body at the same temperature night and day, winter and summer, decade after decade, that Earth's similar ability should be looked upon as serious evidence of her being alive too." We know that innumerable organisms from the lichens that crumble rocks, bacteria that decompose organic matter, the soil that nurtures growth, the oceans that affect temperature, the air that swirls over continents – all of it is a biospheric web of life that is interconnected. Virtually everything draws its character from its relationships with other parts of the ecosphere.[14] Earth, a living world, is so unlike dead planets like Venus and Mars. As Stewart and Lynch observe, "Organisms continually recycle the elements necessary for life as they take in certain chemicals from their environment and expel others, using the atmosphere as a conveyor belt. This gives the atmosphere a highly unlikely chemical signature – one that couldn't be maintained without life."

Life is not just an event happening on Earth; life is fundamental to Earth's existence as a living planet. If alive, is the Earth also sentient? We know nature is more complex and may be more complex than we'll ever know as Barry

Commoner asserted. Perhaps the most modest position one can take is that, "We have no real way of knowing what is sentient and what is not."[15] In a universe of some two hundred billion star families in the Milky Way among other universes, why, in theory at any rate, is there any reason to doubt that life is simply inherent in nature. We know that from its inception as a planet, the Earth has had "Encounters of the extraterrestrial kind…{they} have been a driving force for planetary change since Earth's very life – perhaps even life itself."[16] It may well be that life never began; it was and is always here as a property of the universe. We might consider the possibility that "Spirit is not separate from matter, it is an emergent property of matter."[17] Let's leave this speculative issue and move on to some of the more "earthy" aspects of planet Earth.

Elements

Earth is old, or more accurately, it is middle aged and is in decline. We are in the apogee of the planet's ecological complexity. In the last few decades, scientists have just begun to see how the changes we are forcing on the planet are affecting it. "The equable climate that makes life on Earth possible depends on a hidden web of dynamic connections between ocean, land, and atmosphere… An apparently small change to one part of the system -- such as methane leaking from thawing Siberian bogs – can, through a chain reaction of interlinked processes, have profound global consequences."[18]

The Earth functions best as a finely tuned, balanced and dynamic system linked to and with the air, sea, land, and living entities, all of which are in constant motion. There are feedback loops, and complex connections so fragile as to be scary to those of us beholding them. So far in Earth's history, whatever has been out of balance for any length of time eventually gets back in balance. That may not be the case as long as our supercharged fossil-fuel dominated industrial complex remains on a collision course with the planet. Re-balancing could take as long as a million years or so. "Earth's weather is perhaps the most capricious part of our planet's workings, riven by turmoil, capable of terrible violence, and inclined to strike at random… We tend to think of the air around us as empty space, intangible compared to the fluid feel of water. But in reality air is a fluid too, and just like the ocean the atmosphere is in a continual state of circulation, never still."[19] Consider the hurricane phenomenon and how it develops as it integrates land, sea and air or atmosphere to create a single complex system we dislike so intensely.

One of the unique properties of Earth is that water can exist in all three physical states: vapor, liquid, and as a solid. Without water in liquid form, we could not survive; without water's ability to absorb carbon dioxide from the air and have it flow in the winds of air we would choke; or without the ocean to absorb heat and carbon dioxide, the Earth would not be able to control temperature. We know that the Earth is heating up because of increased temperatures in the sea. "Sea level is a thermometer which indicates the true global warming."[20]

Even though it appears static or stable, ice moves. Artic ice is melting, but like an ice cube in a glass of water, once the ice melts and cools the water, the water once again heats up as it strives for equilibrium. And warm water is not an environment that supports as much life as colder waters. This matters because "About three quarters of all the photosynthesis taking place on Earth occurs in the oceans."[21] and phytoplankton prefer cooler waters. Phytoplankton produce as much of the oxygen in the atmosphere as all the world's forests and jungles combined."[22] Much current knowledge suggests that correcting the imbalance in our oceans has gone beyond repair in our lifetimes. This is yet another case where the re-establishment of the oceans to prehuman conditions could take millions of years.

Guy Murchie reminds us that the tree is a kind of seaweed that learned to live on land, and that the tree is the largest, as well as the longest-living mortal organism on Earth." In James Lovelock's view, the forest of trees "evolved to serve the metabolism of the Earth." Sustainable forests are key to sustainable human life. Opposed to sustainable forests are plantations that are not sustainable. "Sustainable forests are expression of the soil, air, and water – rich, diverse communities coevolving. "Vast open stretches of monoculture farmland are no substitute for natural ecosystems."[23]

I've left out of this discussion the powers of the winds to move the air and assorted particles around the globe as well as the sea currents that alter the weather and climate on the various continents. There is much that could be said about the effect of these systems; however, for now, I simply wanted to make clear that all the elements that make up our ecosystem have roles to play and all of them are being threatened.

Relationships

There is a very strong individualistic strain running through western civilization, one that ignores what is patently obvious to any who are paying attention. We are connected to much more than the individualistic ego acknowledges. Gregory Bateson reminds us that, " We imagine that the unit of survival is the separate individual or a separate species, whereas in reality through the history of evolution, it is the individual plus the environment, the species plus the environment, for they are essentially symbiotic."[24] "All things – objects and beings – exist only interdependently, not independently."[25]

A common view is that we live on the planet. While that is true from one perspective, we do well to acknowledge that we also live within Gaia, the Earth. After all, the atmosphere that we breath, think, act, and are otherwise engaged in is an extension of the functioning planet. We are, as it were, nestled within Earth's bosom and would die without its support. So, in addition to seeing the Earth as more than a resource to exploit at will, we need to see it for what it is: a life-support system. This change in perception reflects a kind of respectful communication between human life and the larger organism of which we are a part. Rather than seeing ourselves as stewards of nature, we are really just other members of the life community, a point that James Lovelock made when he wrote, "We are no more qualified to be the steward or developers of the Earth than are goats to be gardeners,"[26] Within this more-or-less ecocentric view of being participants in the world of nature, "We recognize the inherent value of all other beings, but also the value of their participation in our life."[27]

Too often those concerned with the health of the planet moralize extensively. "Do this, do that. Give up this, give up that," and so on. "Make sacrifices!" It does get tiresome. Instead of all that preaching, perhaps if there was a change in perception, all of that could simply vanish. As Arne Naess suggested, if "The {perception of the} self were widened and deepened so that the protection of nature was felt and perceived as protection of our very self… we {might} realize that the world is our body."[28] With that realization, perhaps more people would see that there need not be a false separation between the Earth and self. And that as we are spiritual as well as physical so, too, is the Earth from which we are born and sustained. Perhaps we could see what Sulak Sivaraksa was getting at when she wrote, that we can't really "separate politics from spirituality, the animal world from the human, or art from the crafts necessary for survival."[29] That we might understand is that in reality, compassion for the condition of the Earth is a measure of our own humanity. For all of that, we do well to heed the caution of Bill Devall when he notes, "Some people say, 'I love the Earth. I want to help all living beings.' But such statements are abstractions… Perhaps a few extraordinary people can develop such an identification, but I suspect most of us have much difficulty understanding the entire Earth. We can relate only with a few beings in our lifetime. We have long term intimate relationships with a few people – our spouse, the other members of our family, our parents, perhaps a few close friends maintained over many years, and a house pet. We understand the universal through the specific."[30] Experientially, our own, personal connection with the Earth is what best informs us, not abstractions, slogans, or even noble beliefs. Again, "The process of maturing as a human involves a gradual widening of one's identification, or self realization… actually experiencing our self differently."[31]

Every day each of us breathes freely and thinks no more of breath than we do the air we breathe, yet it is a function that we do well to attend, as so many spiritual practices insist. It is essential to our existence, as we know, yet we pretty much take it for granted. If one pays attention, it becomes obvious we can smell and actually taste the atmosphere in the course of our breathing. Not only that, but it becomes possible to see the very air we breathe so freely connects us to the spiritual as well. As Jeremy Hayward reminds us, "Spirit… is simply another word for the air, the wind, or the breath. The atmosphere is the spirit, the subtle awareness of this planet. We all dwell within the spirit of the Earth, and this spirit circulates within us. Our individual psyches, our separate subjectivities are all internal expressions of the invisible awareness of the air, the psyche of this world."

Short of transforming our understanding and connection with Gaia, we risk continuing our unconscious attitudes and behavior toward nurturing Gaia that Homer-Dixon raised when he wrote, "The main evidence of our existence on the planet will probably be damage to Earth's life and environment."[32] The fact of the matter, to return to the patient we saw at the beginning of this piece, is that the Earth will continue, change and do what it needs to survive, perhaps over millions of years, but we may not because we will have destroyed the very source that supports our lives, Gaia itself.

Emerging issues

One of the most common experiences many of us have is, "I didn't see it coming!" That is especially the case regarding the fact that consuming needs of western industrial civilization is completely at odds with the limits of the natural world. We appear to be addicted to economic growth at any cost, especially if the price is invisible. Except for a few prescient thinkers back when, this realization – that industrialization pits us against the natural world -- did not begin to surface until early in the twentieth century. As a society, we have been dangerously ignorant of our own ignorance. We have become aware of the collision course we're on as subsequent studies of the deleterious effects of our lifestyle have come into popular consciousness. Further, as we have become aware of the huge issues facing us regarding climate change, there is a tendency to look for a quick fix. We haven't found one, short of considering what would happen if a major volcanic eruption occurred and cooled off the atmosphere. No, the problems we've created are likely to get worse. Not only that, but the likelihood of quick change and surprise is far more likely than our experiencing a slow and gradual environmental degradation. As James Lovelock observed, "You may think that climate and economic forecast have little in common, but they do: both systems are complex and non-linear and can change suddenly and unexpectedly." Or to use another metaphor, think of the cars in a traffic jam – moments of slight movement, then paralysis before moving again in a process that seems never to end. Driving becomes one of fits and starts. Crispin Tickell sums the matter up: "Looking at the global ecosystem as a whole, human population increase, degradation of land, depletions of resources, accumulation of wastes, pollution of all kinds, climate change, abuses of technology, and destruction to biodiversity in all its form together constitute a unique threat to human welfare unknown to previous generations."[33]

The extinction of species is an example. Stewart & Lynch in *Earth, A Biography*, pointed out, "It is ironic that just as we begin to understand how fundamental life is to the working of our planet, we are systematically wiping out the very biodiversity that make Earth such a special, possibly unique, world…. Nearly 16,000 species are now on the brink of extinction… One estimate has it that 30,000 species are indeed disappearing every year." That is a stunning number of extinctions!

For most of us, especially in urban areas, there is little or no sense of loss because the loss of all this life hardly touches us, but to those who are studying the extinction phenomenon up close and personal, the pain of loss is profound. They are aware of what is being lost forever and are aware that we have crossed an irreversible threshold. The difference between those who see the loss and its consequences and those who don't serves as an emblem of the issue. The degree that people are even aware of the issue is limited. "Public perception of the ecological crisis, for the most part, is still at the level of environmentalism. It is limited to attempts at environmental cleanup, to the Greening of consumerism, and to allegedly sustainable growth. Business is pretty much as usual, painted a pale shade of Green."[34] In a way, the polluted environment is a reflection of a polluted understanding. We keep pumping out pollution too fast for natural systems to keep up, and so much information is coming at us all the time we have difficulty staying clear. As one writer put it, "Our world is caught up in a vicious cycle. The more development there is, the more problems appear – and faster than they can be solved. The technocrats cannot stop the spirally monster because they are afraid that if they do, everything will come to a standstill, or the system will go haywire and plunge us all into financial ruin."[35]

Part of the problem is that the fossil fuel dependent system we have created can't be powered down without crashing. And who wants a crash? What seems to be needed is some plan that involves retreating in some way from our currently unsustainable lifestyle. But even that is problematic because "We are so obsessed with the idea of progress and with the betterment of humanity that we regard retreat as a dirty word, something to be ashamed of."[46] No matter, we don't have lots of time and we really do have to do something; maybe one policy could be to reduce our emissions and generating much-needed electricity for the urban areas using –gulp! – nuclear energy which is much cleaner than coal, oil, or gas. There are other options to reduce our contamination of the Earth, of course, but not many. If we don't do something and reasonably soon, we will be the ones who suffer the consequences. As Stewart and Lynch remind us, "So, all this stuff about 'saving planet Earth.' That's nonsense. That's not the problem Planet Earth doesn't need saving. For 4.5 billion years, Earth as been a survivor. It's not the planet we should be worrying about. It's us."

Earth endnotes

1.   Stewart & Lynch, 2007, p. 39.

2.   Martin Rees, in Lovelock, James, <u>The Vanishing Face of Gaia: A Final Warning</u> (2009), Allen Lane, Penguin Books, UK, p. xi.

3.   Stewart & Lynch, 2007, p. 163.

4.   Stewart & Lynch, 2007, p. 57.

5.   Hancock, Graham, <u>Magicians Of The Gods</u> (2015), Coronet Pub, UK, p. 91.

6.   Hancock, 2105, p.431.

7.   Needleman, Jacob, <u>An Unknown World: Notes on The Meaning of The Earth</u> (2012), Jeremy P. Tarcher/Penguiun, NY 2, p. 118.

8.   Stewart & Lynch, 2007, pp. 113 & 115.

9.   Hancock, Graham, <u>Supernatural: Meetings With the Ancient Teachers of Mankind</u> (2005), Doubleday Canada, p. 479.

10.   Stewart & Lynch, 2007, p. 47.

11.   Lovelock, James, <u>The Vanishing Face of Gaia: A Final Warning</u> (2009), Allen Lane, Penguin Books, UK, p. 62.

12.   Lovelock, 2006, p. 62.

13.   Lovelock, 2006, p. 17.

14. Abram, David, <u>The Spell of the Sensuous: Perception and Language in a More-Than-Human World</u> (1997), Vintage Books, NY, p. 85.

15. William LaFleur, Satttva: Enlightenment for Plants and Trees, in Badiner, <u>Allan Hunt, editor, Dharma Gaia: A Harvest of Essays in Buddhism and Ecology</u>, (1990) Parallax Press, Berkeley, CA, p. 137.

16. Stewart & Lynch, 2007, p. 31.

17. Eisenstein, Charles, <u>The Ascent of Humanity: Civilization and the Human Sense of Self</u> (2007), Evolver Editions, North Atlantic Books, Berkeley, CA, p. 384.

18. Stewart & Lynch, 2007, p. 12.

19. Stewart & Lynch, 2007, p. 124.

20. Lovelock, 2009, p. 27.

21. Murchie, 1978, p. 39.

22. Stewart & Lynch, 2007, p. 172.

23. Lovelock, 2006, p. 12.

24. Macy, Joanna, quoted in The Greening of the Self in Badiner, 1990, p. 59.

25. Macy, Joanna, The Greening of the Self in Badiner, 1990, p. xvi).

26. Lovelock, 2006, p. 137.

27.   Deicke, Carla, Women and Ecocentricity,in Badiner, 1990, p. 166.

28.   Macy, Joanna The Greening of the Self in Badiner, 1990, p. 62.

29.   Sivaraksa, Sulak, True Development, in Badiner, 1990, p. 176).

30.   Devall, Bill, Ecocentric Sangha, in Badiner, 1990, pp. 157-158).

31.   Hayward, Jeremy, Ecology and the experience of Sacredness, in Badiner, 1990, p. 64)

32.   Homer-Dixon, Thomas, <u>The Upside of Down: Catastrophe, Creativity, and the Renewal of Civilization</u> (2007), Homer-Dixon, Thomas, Vintage Canada, Toronto, Canada, p. 305.

33.   Tickell, Crispin, in Lovelock, 2006, p. xii

34.   Jones, Ken, Getting Out of Our Own Light, in Badiner, 1990, p. 183.

35.   Sivaraksa, Sulak, True Development, in Badiner, 1990, p. 169.

36.   Lovelock, 2006, p. 7.

7

Community

Chances are that you are already in one or two
communities, some literally in your immediate geographic
area, some virtually in digital space. In matters
environmental, both communities matter. We can act locally
and think globally as the bumper sticker admonishes. But
our global thoughts, values, and attitudes do matter in ways
that are different from what is possible in our local
environment. There is no need to go into any detail about
what each of us can do locally to contribute to awareness of
our precarious global position *vis a vis* Gaia; the chances are
that you are already acting as a global citizen in this matter.
What is different about the virtual community is that we are
affecting what is going on in the world with our quiet (and
sometimes not so quiet) actions, with our sensibilities attuned
to a fresh perspective, and with our values. In a virtual
community, time and space play a minor roll.   From the
virtual community, we collect the dots that matter; in our
personal space, we connect them.[1] In both communities, we
create something akin to small bits of cultural understanding
that are transmitted through – for want of a better word -- the
ethers. As Eric Weiner reminds us, "Culture is social DNA.

116

It transmits traditions from one generation to the next, largely invisibly to us… We behave in certain ways because of this invisible social DNA." We often do not see the effect we are having on others, but it is there. Lynn McTaggart, in *The Intention Experiment* has documented how our thoughts can bring about healing changes in medical patients over long distances. And Dean Radin in *The Conscious Universe* has documented the effect of thoughts on random number generators around the world. Thoughts do matter; our connection to others in the virtual community does have an effect beyond what we consciously think.

Sometimes the forces aligned against any meaningful change in the dominant view of the Earth as simply a resource to be depleted seem overwhelming. That vision of reality may suggest we give up the struggle to re-make our society to work harmoniously with Gaia. It suggests that we are much too small and insignificant a force to alter the resource-depletion paradigm we are currently engaged in.

But that is only one view.

Yes, the western industrial resource depletion war machine sensibility is dominant and challenges anyone seeking a reasonable alternative. And yes, there is an alternative, however, it requires another sensibility, another approach to creating meaning and purpose. We need to remember that our small daily acts, however seemingly insignificant, are our positive contribution to the larger community of living things. As Margaret Mead observed, "Never doubt that a small group of thoughtful, committed individuals can change the world. In fact, it's the only thing that ever has." Each of us is always expressing our values and every action we take is having some effect we may never see. When we are aligned with the energy that moves throughout the Earth, we are subtly nurtured and supported because "The sharing of knowledge, whether between humans or between animals and humans, is nearly always associated with love, caring, and compassion."[2] Further, people get more than emotional satisfaction when engaged in aligning with a larger purpose or being connected to something greater than the self; life fills with meaning and purpose. As Vaclav Havel wrote so clearly, "The salvation in this human world lies nowhere else than in the human heart. . . Without a global revolution in the sphere of human consciousness, nothing will change for the better in the sphere of our being as humans, and the catastrophe toward which this world is headed – be it ecological, social, demographic or a general breakdown of civilization -- will be unavoidable. If we are no longer threatened by world war or by the danger that the absurd mountains of accumulated nuclear weapons might blow up the world, this does not mean that we have definitely won. We are still capable of understanding that the only genuine backbone of all our actions, if they are to be moral, is responsibility: responsibility to something higher than my family, my country, my company, my success – responsibility to the order of being where all our actions are indelibly recorded and where and only where they will be properly judged... Transcendence is the only real alternative to extinction."

Anyone who has experienced a sense of community knows its value and misses the connections when alienated from that community. We like living in groups. It appears it is in our nature to be a part of a group. It may well be that because of evolution, even as babies we seek other humans with whom to engage. We also categorize others into groups. Groups shape our perceptions and as David Abram notes, "We see and hear and otherwise experience very largely as we do because the language habits of our community predispose certain choices of interpretation." Just being a part of a group influences how we feel about others in other groups as well as how we feel about ourselves. To a huge degree, we are a product of those around us and those to whom we pay attention. Usually bland conformity informs our behavior, but "When we conform, it is not so much the power of the group or peer pressure that shapes our behavior. But rather our desire to be accepted."[3] Being accepted in our community appears to affect our immune response as well. Group belonging supports our ability to be healthy and whole. It is clear that when we participate in the health of the Earth, we are helping ourselves and consolidating our sense of community.

For a variety of reasons, many of us have lost community and group connections that were healthy and supportive. A moment's reflection will reveal the power of connecting to center us in our feeling of completeness with those at work, school, family, and so on. Because so many of us have become specialized in the workplace and detached from where we live as we commute, engaging with a local community has become largely incompatible with wage earning. One consequence of that shift is that for many of us, if we feel connected to any community at all, it is with those with whom we work. For many, it is in the workplace that we feel some sense of intimacy with our fellows; the workplace is where we experience intimate connection with others. Given the power of the workplace in the formation of group-belonging or community, the work we choose affects more than the paycheck we take home. Our workplace is our home away from home; it becomes our local literal community.

When we are in the absence of any sort of community feeling, we miss out on a necessary feeling of co-creation and participation in a world we want to make real. Echoing Vaclav Havel, James Braden noted, "It's only when we feel that we're a part of something bigger than ourselves, and can identify where we fit and how we contribute to the 'bigger something,' that our existence in the world and life make sense. In the absence of such meaning, the events of life, including our family relationships, our loves, our jobs, careers, joys, disappointments, failures, and successes, all appear random and disconnected from one another and from us."[5]

There are substitutes that attempt to act as an alternative for community. Being consumers often attempts to replace a sense of community, but as Charles Eisenstein noted, "Consumption calls upon no one's gifts, calls forth none of anyone's true being. Community and intimacy cannot come from joint consumption, but only from giving and co-creativity... Community is woven from gifts."[11] Our inherent gregariousness insists that we need others to help us find meaning in our lives and solo shopping doesn't quite fit the bill. To redress this condition, the suggestion made throughout this book is that by embracing a fresh worldview, one based on kindness and one that respects the Earth and others in an I-Thou relationship, we can recognize the larger human community of which we are all a part. Simple daily behavior can be our ticket out of alienation and lack of community participation and into admission to a world community of care, consideration, and love. While this is not going to be easy, we can do it. As Lynn McTaggart suggests, "We have to do nothing less… than wipe the entire hard drive of our competitive mindset clean."[7] Inherent in this view is the notion that whatever we bring into the world will have to work for everyone. Lest anyone think this is much too difficult and unrealistic, we need to remember that "Co-creation does not mean service as the sacrifice of Self; it means service through the actualization of Self. Self-actualization occurs when we find our vocations and express them meaningfully in the world. Our vocations are drawn forth by the process of finding others we need to work with, by enlivening our individual lives and the quality of life in our communities."[8] It is precisely this absence of self-actualization in the service of some higher purpose that is the appropriate corrective to the corrosive effect of our current lifestyle, a lifestyle that is at odds with creating a sustainable beautiful Earth. A new, fresh perspective is called for, one that addresses what is so endemic and chronic, given our current reality. As Homer-Dixon reminds us, "Depression, depending upon how it is measured, has become three to ten times more common in the past fifty years... Researchers have suggested many explanations, but repeatedly they highlight a cluster of factors: the erosion of community and family, economic culture that promotes chronic insecurity and extreme individualism, unattainable standards of beauty (especially for women), and an overwhelming proliferation of consumer options – because for a surprising number of people an abundance of options doesn't produce happiness but instead acute stress and feelings of inadequacy."[14] We are well-beyond the time to ditch empty acts of consumerism, mindless electronic entertainment, frenetic engagement with the daily news and other diversions. We know we benefit from uninterrupted time, "for pastimes like writing, reading, dancing, gardening, playing a sport or musical instrument, or playing with our children – that bring us real happiness."[10] In short, we need to reconnect with others and the Earth – at work or in our lives in some meaningful way because having them in our lives is really, really good for us. Having a virtual community connects us to so many others who are as concerned with issues as we are.

Political parties know we are all connected. Every time there is an election, all the major issues and the quiet invisible issues come out and demand a hearing and action.

The concerns of the community become quite obvious. In a very different way, those with a sense of urgency about the condition of Gaia make their concerns known by their daily life. They live knowing what they think, feel, and do has a significant, if distant, effect on Gaia's health. It could be called a quantum understanding.

Community endnotes

1. Weiner, Eric The Geography of Genius: A Search for the World's Most Creative Places From Ancient Athens to Silicon Valley (2016), Simon & Schuster, NY, p. 255.

2. Dossey, Larry, One Mind (2011), Hay House Inc. Carlsbad, CA, p. 55.

3.   Hood, Bruce, The Self Illusion: How the Social Brain Creates Identity (2012), HarperCollins Pub. Ltd, Toronto, Canada, p. 197.

4. Weller, Francis, The Wild Edge of Sorrow: Rituals of Renewal and the Sacred Work of Grief (2015), North Atlantic Books, Berkeley, CA, p. 73.

5. Braden, Gregg, The Turning Point: Creating Resilience in a Time of Extremes (2014), Hay House, NY, NY., pp. 123-124.

6. Eisenstein, Charles, Sacred Economics: Money, Gift & Society In The Age OF Transition (2011), North Atlantic Books, Evolver Edition, Berkeley, CA, p. 78.

7. McTaggart, Lynne, Our New Story: Recognizing the Bond, in Hubbard, Barbara, Marx, Birth 2012 And Beyond: Humanity's Great Shift to the Age

of Conscious Evolution (2012), Shift Books,, p. 186.

8. Hubbard, 2012, p. 82.

9. Homer-Dixon, Thomas, The Upside of Down: Catastrophe, Creativity, and the Renewal of Civilization (2007), Homer-Dixon, Thomas, Vintage Canada, Toronto, Canada, p. 198.

10. Homer-Dixon, 2007, p. 197.

8
Intelligence

We intuitively know that intelligence is all around us. Take the common phrase, "The weather has a mind of its own" as an example. Or the changes in the seasons signaled by the turning of leaves or the thickness of a caterpillar's coat that are the stuff of the *Farmer's Almanac*. Or that pet owners know their pets have intelligence; or that researchers know that plants have a way of being that seems to indicate intelligence; or the sublime order of planetary motion that has fascinated astronomers forever. Somewhere in all of this is the question, "Is the universe intelligent as well?"

A definition of intelligence appears to be in order. However, that definition varies according to whom it is asked. As a case in point, when two dozen notable psychology theoreticians were asked for a definition of intelligence, they came up with two dozen definitions. Yet, for all the discreet differences in definition, there is a general consensus as to what constitutes intelligence. According to psychologist Alfred Binet, "It is not merely book learning, a narrow academic skill, or test-taking smarts. Rather, it reflects a broader and deeper capability for comprehending our surroundings." For the purposes of this discussion, let's just say we all have an understanding (more or less) of what constitutes intelligence generally and we (again, more or less) know intelligence when we observe it in others, our earthly environment, our pets, and in plant life. So, even though we can't definitively prove intelligence in non-human forms of life, we know as a practical matter it exists. As Michael A. Cremo in Human Devolution reminds us, "Initial assumptions must simply be reasonable on the basis of available evidence."

While there are some examples of scientific support for the idea that consciousness or intelligence exists outside human experience, here we are essentially looking at the issue from the point of view of meaning, "Why does this exist?" rather than the strictly scientific perspective, which is concerned with "What makes it do that?" Both questions are valid, of course, but each asks different questions to derive different answers. It may well be that the universe is speaking to us endlessly, as Primack and Abrams note. "People ask the universe the questions they are capable of conceiving and hear the answers they are capable of hearing."[1] For example, we all know we are made of atoms. That is a scientific cliché. But "there is no humanness to our atoms. Whether atoms are inside us, inside a rock, or drifting through space, is all the same to them. On the atomic scale, therefore, even inside our own bodies we do not exist. "We" are something that transcends atoms."[2] We are made of rather common elements, elements that have been around since before the very beginning of evolution. Somehow we are more than the elements that we are composed of. We seem to be designed to inquire about our purpose and the purpose of everything else. We might say that, "The universe itself may have been designed for human life and other forms of life. The evidence supports the assumption that humans not only were designed to be inquirers, they were placed in an exceptionally well-suited position from which to inquire."[3]

Each of us is – at some level -- a walking history of the universe. We come from an almost inconceivable past in the universe and carry that history in our very bones. Or as one scientist put it, "Because we are made of the same stuff as the universe, we can experience our interconnectedness with the universe."[4] The philosopher, Alan Watts, put the matter this way. "We say, 'I came into this world.' But we did nothing of the kind. We came out of it in just the same way the fruit comes out of trees. Our galaxy, our cosmos, "peoples" in the same way that an apple tree "apples."[5]

Before going further, let's digress for a moment and consider a couple of notions. In the history of ideas, let's remember as we go along that new ideas or fresh ways of looking at things usually don't get a lot of good press. The trouble is that "Belief is a social phenomenon. With rare exceptions, we cannot hold our beliefs without reinforcement from people around us. Beliefs that deviate substantially from the general social consensus are especially hard to maintain, requiring usually some kind of sanctuary."[6]

Stepping out of a belief system is difficult. This is commonly understood in the statement that every journey begins with a first step, but what is less commonly understood is that what it takes to make that first step is often the hardest part of the process. An oft-quoted statement from philosopher Arthur Schopenhauer has it that, "All truth passes through three stages. First, it is ridiculed. Second, it is violently opposed. Third, it is accepted as being self-evident." Dean Radin, often at the forefront of cutting edge research in psi phenomena, gets to the same idea using four stages for the acceptance of new ideas:

1. The idea is impossible.
2. The idea is possible, but not worth the time.
3. The idea is better than previous thought.
4. Original skeptics say they came up with the idea in the first place.

With that understanding in mind, let's proceed to explore our relationship to "all that is." It has been said that humans "Are mysterious beings of mysterious origins." To understand our relationship with "all that is," perhaps there is something valid in the ancient wisdom from the Vedas that will help us out. These Sanskrit writings tell us that there is a realm of pure consciousness that bathes and permeates the entire cosmos. The Vedas call this energy Akasha. However, because this energy is so subtle, our bodies cannot register it except through spiritual practice, if at all. Recent scientific findings confirm the fact that we are surrounded and bathed in a "field of energy that cannot be seen, heard, touched, tasted or smelled. However this field produces effects, and these can be perceived."[7] The Vedas and current science appear to be in agreement. Ervin Laszlo goes on to note, "Both matter and mind – *physis* as well as *psyche* – are omnipresent in the universe. They were present even when the universe was born." Matter and mind are different aspects of the same reality. And from Dean Radin, who has studied aspects of this other world notes, "Underlying the isolated world of ordinary objects and human experience is another reality, an interconnected world of intermingling relationships and possibilities. This underlying reality is more fundamental—in the sense of being the ground state from which everything originates — than the transient forms and dynamic relationships of familiar experience."

One of the early twentieth century theoretical physicists to be aware of the existence of a reality usually unknown to most of us is David Joseph Bohm who wrote of the explicate and implicate order. Greg Braden explains what these terms refer to. "The things that we can see and touch and that appear separate in our world – such as rocks, oceans, forests, animals, and people – are examples of the explicate order of creation. However, as distinct as they may appear from one another, Bohm suggested that they're linked in a deeper reality in ways that we simply cannot see from our place in creation. He viewed all of the things that look separate to us as part of a greater wholeness, which he called the implicate order…What we see as our world is actually the projection of something even more real that's happening at a deeper level of creation. It is this deeper level that's the original – the implicate."[8]

You may find all of this a bit too removed from ordinary perception. Here it may be useful to heed Guy Murchee's advice. He wrote, "We must unsense some things in order to sense other things. The fact that only when it is dark can you see the stars is thus reconciled to the fact that only when you lose some senses do you become aware of others."[9] All of which is to say that rather than blindly dismissing these fields as unreal, we would do well to acknowledge that they exist on a plane of reality that is not the same as the plane of observation. Simply put, there is more than one plane of existence but the universe is One and we are part and parcel of it. At the very least, one can say that, "If the universe is not intelligent in itself, it contains intelligences."[10]

Let's digress a moment.

You and I have a long history. We are somewhere in the vicinity of 4.5 billion years in the making. That's when life on Earth began, more or less. With such a pedigree, you may regard yourself as at least a little bit special; so do I. As two science writers noted, "The history of the universe is in every one of us. Every particle in our bodies has a multibillion-year past, every cell and every bodily organ has a multimillion-year past, and many of our ways of thinking have multi-thousand-year pasts. Each of us is a kind of nerve center where these various cosmic histories intersect."[11]

If, on the other hand, we aren't at all special, are we an accident of evolution, an anomaly that doesn't fit anywhere or in any way in the grand scheme of things, or just a bunch of atoms strewn together that have no point or purpose beyond perpetuating the species? At some point, the question has to be asked, "Is there a point to our having a life that may be related to the evolution of the Earth and the universe?" Answers to this question differ considerably.

Existentialists claim there is no intrinsic purpose to your life unless you create such a purpose. Materialistic philosophers see the universe as a mechanism that has no purpose; it simply exists and will eventually disappear in the same way your death will disappear you. The post modernists argue there is no story, no myth that isn't relative or more true than anything else. Religionists of one sort or another argue there is "some pleasant place" (if we behave ourselves according to the rules laid down by the particular religion) that we all go to eventually. Beyond these somewhat dismal choices, is there any other option regarding our place in the scheme of things?

Perhaps there is.

And to get to that option, we have to look at a controversial idea that, on the face of it, doesn't seem all that complicated. It comes down to a question of design. But before looking at that question, you may want to reflect on your life now. You were born, did all the things along the way that brought you to exactly where you are now. The question is, "Did you consciously design your life or have you more-or-less stumbled into what your life is now?" And "Could you have predicted the life you now have?"

For many of us -- perhaps most, if not all -- the answers are fairly clear. Whatever other qualities you possess, you have intelligence. You worked with the world you inherited. You may not have consciously designed the life you now have, but the design of your life followed from the intelligence you have and the material and social world you live in. What is clear is that you likely did not have a prior specific design for where you are now. In short, design of your life may have evolved simply from the daily use of your intelligence. The ultimate design of your life may not have been exactly the result of a purposeful, planned or specific idea; the life you have came out of the working of your intelligence as it developed; your life was being designed as it evolved. You wound up here.

Perhaps the universe operates in the same way. A deep intelligence may exist within the universe, an intelligence that is sentient and is in operation all the time. That intelligence worked with the materials at hand. It created the universe as we know it. That intelligence created complex systems. And what we know about complex systems is that, "Complex systems are more likely to produce what scientists call an emergent phenomenon… An emergent phenomenon represents a new kind of order created from an old system."[12] One might say this is design in the making.

This emergent system, like the universe, always had consciousness. As Peter Russell notes, "Whatever consciousness we have, it has to have come from the cosmos and been inherited by us. We know we have consciousness and it appears to me that it must be in and of the Earth itself in some form as well. Where else would it have come from?"[13] Considering the evolving universe as intelligent is consistent with current scientific understanding; the same principles operate. Including intelligence as inherent in matter allows us to account for human consciousness and intelligence without having to insist that consciousness and intelligence are epiphenomena, a purely secondary effect of matter – a logical impossibility. That is to say, trying to explain how something like consciousness and intelligence can come from inert matter is eliminated. Consciousness is always present.

The characteristics of an emergent system are unpredictable. How would any intelligence – think about how you wound up here -- know in advance what a new emergent system would be like? (Parenting is an emergent system. Ask any parent if they really knew what life actually would be like with children.) The universe as a living system, like us, does what it does. It produces complex systems that in turn produce unknowable outcomes. Imagine this process going on for billions of years and eventually producing everything in the universe and our place in it. We are sentient, conscious, intelligent because the universe from which the Earth was created has all of these characteristics. The earth's elements and dynamic forces (originally derived from the cosmos) then provided the environment for the development all the additional stuff on the planet, including all life and its manifestations. Remember, though, the Earth's stuff and characteristics, however unique, ultimately evolved from the universe. It might be said that the universe is the parent of the Earth and all the other planets. In this view, the Earth is but one child of many. The Earth will always share certain aspects of itself with its source, the universe. The Earth and all that is contained within and about it will have intelligence inherited from the universe. How marvelous for humans! As far as we know, life on earth is unique; that is, no other planet has such a creation. How this happened is one of the mysteries of creation.

When conjuring up an image of the universe, some people see remote heavenly spheres swirling about in space. For others the universe is simply empty space. In both cases, there is no place for life itself, no connection with the subtle bond we have with the universe. Going about our daily life, we may find it difficult to envision another perspective, one where it is more accurate to say, "I am what the expanding universe is doing here and now…There is a real dissonance between the colorful, volatile, science-expanded world we actually inhabit and the monotonously recycled language that religions use to describe " ultimate reality."[14] In the words of Charles Eisenstein, "We need to rediscover the mind of nature, to return to our original animism and the ensouled universe it perceived. We need to understand nature, the planet, the sun, the soil, the water, the mountains, the rocks, the trees, and the air as sentient beings whose destiny is not separate from our own... We and the Earth are one… Perhaps all our small, invisible acts imprint themselves upon the world in ways we do not understand."[15] Once a person sees that the whole history of the universe was necessary for each of us to come into existence, a person's attitude regarding how we all fit into the cosmic perspective shifts.

What's more, if we can accept the idea that we are integral to the universe itself, then we can see how we reflect some of the properties of the whole. It could be argued that when we discover our own deeper nature, we will have found the deeper nature of the cosmos. In this line of thinking, a cosmology of a living universe is vital if we are to feel that we belong here and that our existence is purposeful. As we see that we are beings of cosmic connection who are learning to live in a vibrant universe, we are motivated to live more sustainably on the Earth and compassionately with one another. Further, since the foundation of the universe is alive, it makes sense that from life emerges further life. In this view, aliveness is both fundamental and emergent -- it is both permeating and sustaining the foundations of the universe, as well an emergent property of self-organizing systems that have the capacity to reflect upon themselves. In the words of Erwin Laszlo, "In the great chain of evolution, there is nowhere we can draw the line, nowhere we could say: below this there is no consciousness, and above there is... The higher forms of knowing, such as human awareness and intention, have their roots in the cosmos; they were there in potential at the birth of the universe." Having a view that takes as its assumption that the Earth and the universe of which it is a part have meaning and value is helpful if we want to maintain mental and physical health personally and socially.

I can think of no better way to end this discussion than taking the words of Eisenstein to heart when he writes, "The spontaneous arising of order, beauty, and life that is written into the laws of the universe, and even more deeply, into the structure of mathematics, that is repeated in every nonlinear system with certain very general characteristics, and that it is like that only because it is like that and could be no other way, is far more awesome. I offer the reader not a mundane universe in which nothing is sacred because there is no God, nor a split universe in which some things are holy, of God, and others just matter, but rather a universe which is fully sacred, pregnant with meaning, immanent with divinity, in which order, organization, and beauty arise spontaneously from the ground up, neither imposed from above by a designer nor projected from within by the observer, and of which God is an inseparable property. The marvelous complexity and beauty of nature is not some consolation prize for science's denial of the sacred, but evidence that the universe is itself sacred."

Thus we end our discussion of our connection with "all that is." Again, while such a perspective may not be commonplace, it is a view that is consistent with having care and concern for our fellow humans, with the ecological systems of the Earth, and with the deep spiritual roots of human consciousness. It is a view well worth considering as we go about reclaiming our role as stewards of the Earth and all of its creatures.

Intelligence endnotes

1. Primack, Joel R, & Abrams, Nancy Ellen, The View From the Center of The Universe (2006), , Riverhead Books, NY. p. 36.

2. Primack and Abrams, p.285.

3. Dentel, Dave, Mysterious Origins – Are Humans Just a Happy Accident? p. 63, in Peet, Preston, ed., Disinformation Guide to Ancient Aliens, Lost Civilizations, Astonishing Archaeology & Hidden History (2005), Disinformation Books, San Francisco, CA.

4. Radin, Dean, The Conscious Universe; The Scientific Truth of, p. 314.

5. Watts, Alan W, The Joyous Cosmology: Adventures in the Chemistry of Consciousness, Second Edition (2013), New World Library, Novato, California. First published in 1962.

6. Eisenstein, Charles, The More Beautiful World Our Hearts Know is Possible (2013), North Atlantic Books, Berkeley, CA., pp. 248-249.

7. Laszlo, Ervin, Science and the Akashic Field: An Integral Theory of Everything, (2007), second edition, Inner Traditions, Rochester, Vermont, p. 73.

8. Braden, Gregg, <u>The Divine Matrix: Bridging Time , Space, Miracles, and Belief.</u> (2007), Hay House Pub, pp. xii & xiii.

9. Murchie, Guy, <u>The Seven Mysteries of Life: An Exploration in Science and Philosophy</u> (1978), Houghton Mifflin Co. Boston, p. 238.

10. Mack, John, E., <u>Conversations on the Edge of the Apocalypse: Contemplating the Future with Noam Chomsky, George Carlin, Deepak Chopra, Rupert Sheldrake, and Others</u> (2005), David Jay Brown, Palgrave MacMillan, Hampshire, England, p. 98.

11. Primack and Nancy Ellen Abrams, Riverhead Books, NY p.151.

12. Weiner, Eric <u>The Geography of Genius: A Search for the World's Most Creative Places From Ancient Athens to Silicon Valley</u> (2016), Simon & Schuster, NY, p. 202.

13. Russell, Peter, Interview in: Martin, Stephan, <u>Cosmic Conversations: Dialogues on the Nature of the Universe and the Search for Reality</u> (2010), Career Press, Franklin Lakes, NJ.

14. Primack and Nancy Ellen Abrams, Riverhead Books, NY p. 269.

15. Eisenstein, 2007, p. 51.

Coda

We live in a world of relationships. Among the most important of these are our relationships with family, friends, work associates, and community members. It is possible that many are aware of the web of relationships in the human realm and treat others more-or-less in an "I-Thou" relationship. (To review quickly: an I-Thou" relationship is one in which I meet you as you are and you meet me as who I am.) An "I-Thou" relationship can refer to a relationship with non-human life and Nature as much as it can refer to the relationship between two individuals.

As suggested, we are also in significant relationship with the Earth and all of its non-human inhabitants, and often treat those entities as an "I-It" or as objects to be dominated and controlled. Perhaps most of us are not aware of the web of non-human relationships that make up our lives. Nonetheless, we are inextricably connected to all of these entities.

Often, we seem to refer to the self as an object, an "I-It", as in "I'm this fat or skinny thing" or " I'm not as intelligent, or successful, or as handsome or pretty as someone else" as we note our imperfections and get into a comparative mindset where we often don't fare well. When

I'm in an intimate "I-Thou" with myself, I am respectful and accepting of the way I am and accord myself an understanding and tolerance I often reserve only for others. This understanding is where personal transformation starts. Once I recognize and value myself, that is, see myself as being in an internal "I-Thou" consciousness, I can then treat others, Nature or the world, or "all that is" as an "I-Thou" relationship.

I've outlined and detailed the position that embraces a return to being in harmony with all the life around us. To see oneself as connected and embedded in Nature, to feel re-united to the world, and to see oneself as an expression of the intelligence of the universe on the planet is a powerful reminder that we belong here and that we are meant to live in harmony with each other and with the planet.

The Earth is a huge and immensely complex self-regulating system. (Some of us see the Earth as alive.) We are utterly and totally dependent upon it remaining self-regulating if we have any hope of surviving as a species. The current and limited approaches to doing the necessary ecological actions are necessary but not sufficient. We need more than the superficial window dressing that is passing for ecological action. A personal transformation in our relationship with the Earth is a good place to start.

This position – to connect with the non-human community and the Earth as a living entity is not a final answer – I don't have one – but it is one place to start that is a sensible approach available to all of us. It is a fairly simple and immediate step anyone can take. That is, it is a first step. All else follows from that.

Connect! celebrated the fact of our existence; *Shift!* extended possibilities in thinking about fresh possibilities; *Relate!* encourages us to choose to own our embeddedness in an enchanted world as the participants in and creatures of the Earth. Embeddedness is our reality. It is a source of joy to see oneself as connected; it enlarges the sense of self.

We can continue to live the way we have for some time to come, that is, we can continue to toxify and contaminate the Earth and displace and destroy the lives of indigenous peoples. We can continue to make the Earth's climate inhospitable. Or we can begin to explore alternatives. The current system has been based on easy access to cheap oil. We lived as if our lifestyle could go on forever. That has not been the reality for some time. An ever-growing and expanding consuming system was not sustainable. In addition, the issue of climate change is clearly affecting everyone. Over time, as our system continues to experience deficiencies using the old model, one based on cheap oil, more and more people will recognize the complete challenge to our current way of life and how the up-coming changes will dramatically affect life as we know it -- or more accurately, civilization as we know it. As the Dalai Lama wrote in *Tibetan Portrait: The Power of Compassion,* "We are at the dawn of an age in which extreme political concepts and dogmas may cease to dominate human affairs. We must use this historic opportunity to replace them with universal human and spiritual values. And ensure that these values become the fiber of the global family which is emerging."

The current incarnation of society is disappearing now and will continue irreversibly. We can continue to live in illusion or we can choose to begin to make the necessary adaptations now and have some sort of control of the process of change.

References

Abram, David, <u>The Spell of the Sensuous: Perception and Language in a More-Than-Human World</u> (1997), Vintage Books, NY.

Anderson, Walter Truett, <u>Reality Isn't What It Used To Be: Theatrical Politics, Ready-to-Wear Religion, Global Myths, Primitive Chic, and Other Wonders of the Postmodern world</u>. (1990), HaperSanFransico, CA.

Anderson, Walter Truett, <u>The Truth About The Truth: De-Confusing and Re-Constructing The Postmodern World</u>, Tarcher/Putnam, NY.

Badiner, Allan Hunt, editor, <u>Dharma Gaia: A Harvest of Essays in Buddhism and Ecology</u>, (1990) Parallax Press, Berkeley, CA.

Baggini, Julian, <u>Philosophy</u> (2012), Hodder Education, London, UK.

Borges, Phil, <u>Tibetan Portrait: The Power of Compassion</u> (1996), Text by His Holiness the Dalai Lama, Rizzoli Intl. Pubs, NY, NY.

Braden, Gregg, <u>Deep Truth: Igniting the Memory of Our origin, History, Destiny, and Fate</u> (2011), Hay House, NY, NY.

Braden, Gregg, <u>The Divine Matrix: Bridging Time , Space, Miracles, and Belief.</u> (2007), Hay House Pub.

Braden, Gregg, <u>The Turning Point: Creating Resilience in a Time of Extremes</u> (2014), Hay House, NY, NY.

Dark Mountain Project, http://dark-mountain.net/about/manifesto/

Dentel, Dave, in Peet, (2005), <u>Mysterious Origins – Are Humans Just a Happy Accident?</u>

Dossey, Larry, <u>One Mind</u> (2011), Hay House Inc. Carlsbad, CA

Eisenstein, Charles, <u>The Ascent of Humanity: Civilization and the Human Sense of Self</u> (2007), Evolver Editions, North Atlantic Books, Berkeley, CA.

Eisenstein, Charles, <u>Sacred Economics: Money, Gift & Society In The Age OF Transition</u> (2011), North Atlantic Books, Evolver Edition, Berkeley, CA.

Eisenstein, Charles, <u>The More Beautiful World Our Hearts Know is Possible</u> (2013), North Atlantic Books, Berkeley, CA.

Goldstein, Rebecca, <u>Plato at The Googleplex: Why Philosophy Won't Go Away</u> (2014), Pantheon Books, NY.

Greer, John Michael, <u>Getting Beyond the Narratives: An Open Letter to the Activist Community</u>, (2005), http://www.ecosophia.net/getting-beyond-narratives/

Hancock, Graham, editor, The Divine Spark (2015), Disinformation Books, San Francisco, CA.

Hancock, Graham, <u>Fingerprints of The Gods</u> (1995), Three River Press, NY.

Hancock, Graham, <u>Magicians Of The Gods</u> (2015), Coronet Pub, UK.

Hancock, Graham, <u>Supernatural: Meetings With the Ancient Teachers of Mankind</u> (2005), Doubleday Canada.

Homer-Dixon, Thomas and Garrison, Nick, <u>Carbon Shift: How the Twin Crises of Oil Depletion and Climate Change Will Define the Future</u> (2009), Random House of Canada.

Homer-Dixon, Thomas, <u>The Upside of Down: Catastrophe, Creativity, and the Renewal of Civilization</u> (2007), Homer-Dixon, Thomas, Vintage Canada, Toronto, Canada.

Hood, Bruce, <u>The Self Illusion: How the Social Brain Creates Identity</u> (2012), HarperCollins Pub. Ltd, Toronto, Canada.

Hubbard, Barbara, Marx, <u>Birth 2012 And Beyond: Humanity's Great Shift to the Age of Conscious Evolution</u> (2012), Shift Books, <u>www.shiftmovement.com</u>.

Klein, Naomi, <u>This Changes Everything: Capitalism vs. The Climate</u> (2014), Alfred A. Knopf, Canada.

Laszlo, Ervin, <u>Science and the Akashic Field: An Integral Theory of Everything</u>, (2007), second edition, Inner Traditions, Rochester, Vermont.

Lovelock, James, <u>The Revenge of Gaia</u> (2006), Penguin Group, London, UK.

Lovelock, James, <u>The Vanishing Face of Gaia: A Final Warning</u> (2009), Allen Lane, Penguin Books, UK.

Martin, Stephan, <u>Cosmic Conversations: Dialogues on the Nature of the Universe and the Search for Reality</u> (2010), Career Press, Franklin Lakes, NJ.

McIntosh, Steve, <u>Integral Consciousness And The Future Of Evolution: How The Integral Worldview Is Transforming Politics, Culture, And Spirituality</u> (2007), Paragon House, St. Paul, MN.

McKay, Tom, <u>NASA Study Concludes When Civilization Will End, And It's Not Looking Good for Us</u>

McTaggart, Lynne, <u>The Bond: Connecting Through The Space Between Us</u> (2011), Free Press, NY.

McTaggart, Lynne. <u>The Intention Experiment: Using Your Thoughts to Change Your Life And The World,</u> Free Press, 2007.

McKenna, Terence, <u>Food of the Gods: The Search For the Original Tree of Knowledge</u> (1992), Bantam Books, NY.

Murchie, Guy, <u>The Seven Mysteries of Life: An Exploration in Science and Philosophy</u> (1978), Houghton Mifflin Co. Boston.

Needleman, Jacob, <u>An Unknown World: Notes on The Meaning of The Earth</u> (2012), Jeremy P. Tarcher/Penguiun, NY.

Nuwer, Rachel, <u>How Western Civilization Could Collapse,</u> (2017) http://www.bbc.com/future/story/20170418-how-western-civilisation-could-collapse

Peet, Preston, ed., <u>Disinformation Guide to Ancient Aliens, Lost Civilizations, Astonishing Archaeology & Hidden History</u> (2005), Disinformation Books, San Francisco, CA.

Pollan, Michael, <u>The Intelligent Plant</u>, The New Yorker, December 23, 2013.

Primack, Joel, R., Abrams, Nancy Ellen, <u>The View From the Center of The Universe</u> (2006), Riverhead Books, NY.

Radin, Dean, <u>The Conscious Universe; The Scientific Truth of Psychic Phenomena</u> (1997), HarperCollins, NY.

Shepard, Paul, <u>Coming Home to the Pleistocene</u> (1998), Edited by Florence R. Shepard, Island Press/Shearwater books, Covelo, CA.

Shepard, Paul, <u>Nature and Madness</u> (1998), University of Georgia Press, Athens, GE.

Stewart, Ian & Lynch, John, <u>Earth: The Biography</u> (2007), National Geographic Society, Washington, DC.

Suzuki, David, " Reflections of an Eco-Warrior", <u>Zoomer</u>, Dec 2017/ Jan 2018, PP. 78-79.

Swan, James A, <u>Sacred Places: How The Living Earth Seeks Our Friendship</u>, (1990), Bear & Company Publishing, Santa Fe, New Mexico.

Weiner, Eric <u>The Geography of Genius: A Search for the World's Most Creative Places From Ancient Athens to Silicon Valley</u> (2016), Simon & Schuster, NY.

Weiner, Eric <u>The Geography of Bliss: One Grump's Search for the Happiest Places in the World</u> (2008), Twelve: Hachette Book Group, NY, NY.

Weiner, Eric, <u>Man Seeks God: My Flirtation With The Divine</u> (2011), Hatchette Book Club, NY.

Weller, Francis, <u>The Wild Edge of Sorrow: Rituals of Renewal and the Sacred Work of Grief</u> (2015), North Atlantic Books, Berkeley, CA.

Wright, Ronald, <u>What Is America? A Short History of the New World Order</u> (2008), Alfred A Knopf, Canada, Toronto, CA.

Wright, Ronald, <u>A Short History of Progress</u> (2004), House of Anansi Press Inc., Toronto, Ontario, Canada.

www.ingramcontent.com/pod-product-compliance
Lightning Source LLC
Chambersburg PA
CBHW021145260726
48656CB00024B/1478